History for
the Average Child

History for the Average Child

suggestions on teaching history to pupils
of average and below average ability

P.H.J.H.GOSDEN and D.W.SYLVESTER
Department of Education, University of Leeds

BASIL BLACKWELL   OXFORD

Printed in Great Britain by Alden & Mowbray Ltd
at the Alden Press, Oxford
and bound by the Kemp Hall Bindery

Contents

List of Plates

Preface

The idea of writing this book arose out of a course of evening meetings on teaching history to pupils of average and less than average ability in secondary schools which was organized by the University of Leeds Institute of Education early in 1967. The large number of teachers who attended these meetings and the interest shown was some indication of the concern felt by many of those who face the problems involved in teaching history to 'Newsom' pupils to the age of 16.

Books about history teaching often commend strongly the teaching of one type of history or one approach to history to the virtual exclusion of all others. In this book we have attempted to set out some of the advantages of a number of varied approaches and to suggest methods and practices which have been found useful in the classroom.

Acknowledgements

We are grateful to all who have helped in the preparation of this book. We are especially indebted to Mr. G. V. Pinnell and to Mr. D. Maw of Dinnington High School, near Sheffield, also to Mr. J. B. Willcock of the West Riding County Inspectorate for their valued help and suggestions.

We would also like to acknowledge the help of the teachers who attended the Leeds Institute of Education course on history teaching last winter; by their questions and contribution to discussions they did much to determine the shape and nature of this book.

1. The Approach to History

'A man who is ignorant of the society in which he lives, who knows nothing of its place in the world and who has not thought about his place in it, is not a free man even though he has a vote. He is easy game for "the hidden persuaders". A society in which he and his like predominate is at their mercy. We may turn Abraham Lincoln's saying to our situation: "this nation cannot survive half slave and half free". Too often, however, the boys and girls with whom we are concerned do not see this. Geography and perhaps even more frequently history lessons are expendable as far as boys, and to a less extent girls are concerned. They cannot buy anything with this kind of knowledge as they can with physics and shorthand; they are not always willing to pay for it with hard work as they will for the skills of handicraft or dressmaking. Henry Ford's "history is bunk", -
did they but know it, expresses exactly what they feel; but, of course, Henry Ford is as dead to them as Queen Anne—or history' (Newsom Report, *Half Our Future*).

This somewhat pessimistic and doubting view of the place and value of history in the curriculum has grown up in recent years as the extension of compulsory secondary schooling has kept—and will keep—in their classrooms an ever increasing number of boys and girls who are not among the most able. A growing awareness of the issues raised by this view has been apparent in the educational press and among teachers during the last few years. This discussion necessarily centres on the purpose of history as part of a general education which is appropriate to the needs of the majority of pupils in the secondary school. Those concerned about the present situation are bound to ask whether the kind of history which is taught in most schools is really serving a valid educational purpose. Is it helping to develop the kind of attitudes and experiences which enable boys and girls to understand the world they live in? If not, what kind of changes might be made so that it can become more valuable and so that the pupils themselves might see and appreciate its relevance to their interests and needs? Would it be helpful if teachers of history came to think of their subject more as a dimension of the whole

1

field of human experience and achievement, than as a body of knowledge in itself? Is it enough simply to change the content of syllabuses in order to make them more relevant? Or is something more fundamental needed?

Before considering these questions further, it might be as well to look more closely at this matter of 'relevance'. It is easy to say that secondary school courses need to achieve a greater relevance, but one must inquire what they are to be relevant to. It is difficult to believe that there is any answer to the problem of making history courses more relevant in the eyes of reluctant pupils simply by exchanging one set of subject matter for another which happens to be more recent. Just to teach the facts of the history of the twentieth century can be as stultifying in educational terms as to teach just the facts of any other century. To replace one set of information by another simply because it may appear to have some more direct usefulness does not necessarily make it more meaningful from the point of view of the children. Making any part of the curriculum have greater relevance in the education of children may have more to do with relating it to their needs, interests and capacities than with revising its content to bring it more up to date. Now in order to do this it is necessary to begin by clarifying one's views and beliefs both about the kind of contribution a study such as history can make to the development of children's ideas and experiences, and also about what the conditions are under which pupils of various ages and abilities can learn. Only after becoming clearer about these two factors is it possible to select subject matter which can provide real and valid educational experiences and to select the most appropriate teaching methods.

What are the contributions which a study of history can make? What opportunities and experiences can it offer from which boys and girls can benefit and gain satisfaction and enjoyment, and which really can enrich and improve their lives? In short, how can this part of the curriculum be justified?

When the subject first began to appear on the curricula of schools in the nineteenth century it was widely regarded as a vehicle for the transmission of moral ideas. A study of the textbooks in common use indicates that much of the purpose of history teaching was to inspire a sense of moral indignation about the 'crimes' of a Napoleon or a Charles I. In the 1848 edition of *Baldwin's History of England* moral judgements are offered boldly 'Henry VIII was of a capricious and unrelenting temper; he governed this country, once so free, and which afterwards reconquered her liberties, like a Turkish Sultan; whomsoever of his subjects he had a dispute with, he put to death'. Again the widely read historical books for children associated with the name of Mrs. Trimmer offer what really amount to moral judgements in a historical context. *A Short History of France* of 1819 states that: 'On the 11th of December 1792, the king was brought to the bar of the National Convention and underwent a sort of mock trial, where he was accused of being a sort of enemy to his country, and as such, condemned to death. The persons who thus devoted their king to the scaffold, were most of them of the lowest orders of the people, and distinguished only by their crimes: excepting the duke d'Orleans, a man of a most profligate and wicked character, who joined the republican party, and voted for the death of his sovereign and near relation, in hopes, probably, that he might eventually have been placed by his party on the throne. . . .'

'However dreadful in their details, or awful in their consequences, such great revolutions are, it must be remembered that the steps to them are generally slow and silent: most commonly luxury and corruption of morals are their primary causes; and when nations have reached a certain point of vice and immorality, the Almighty Ruler of the universe "sends forth the power of his wrath" for their chastisement and reformation. The virtuous few must then be involved in the direful events necessary for the correction of a guilty nation. Let those who escape these heavy judgements be grateful to that Power which preserves them; remembering that national crimes are the sins of individuals, and that it is the duty of every subject to consider how far his own particular conduct may contribute to the prosperity or chastisement of his country.'

The fostering of a sense of loyalty and pride in country and Empire went along with the moral teaching and became, perhaps, more pronounced as the century advanced. Although this is now a somewhat outmoded and unfashionable view in this country, the use of the teaching of history to inculcate various political creeds and ideas remains widespread in the contemporary world. Later on attention focused on ideas of cause and effect, on trends and movements and on the assumption of the inevitability of progress.

In recent years a good deal of stress has been laid upon the importance of learning to weigh evidence and to discriminate between fact and opinions. Good history teaching certainly tries to

3

embody these particular aims, for history in the secondary school is one of the most important of those subjects which can help towards the achievement of three main needs which are central to general education, namely:

To help boys and girls to understand themselves better;
To help them develop their ability to understand and respond to other people;
To help them build their understanding of the communities and societies in which they live.

In the first place, history is about people, it is an important part of the record of man's experience, ambition, problems and achievements, and together with other elements in the curriculum such as literature, geography and religious knowledge, a large part of its contribution to education is that it can extend the pupil's experience and understanding of people, their actions and their motives. A considerable part of the understanding of history depends on the imaginative reconstruction of another person's point of view and in their study of history children should be constantly asked to make this act of the imagination, to capture another person's feelings, to recognize his thoughts and to interpret his motives. This is a fundamental element of historical thought; this ability to understand another person is also fundamental to social life. To be able to appreciate how another person is likely to feel, to react and to act in a given situation, to be aware of other people in this sense, to have a concern for them and a willingness to allow for differences in point of view—these form the basis for the mutual relationships of members of a community. For boys and girls in secondary schools, history can be a very fruitful and important means of encouraging the development of this capacity of sympathetic imagination. Through the development of this form of insight into human beings, this search for a meaningful understanding of human activity, the child not only comes to know more about other people, he also comes to know more about himself. The development of this quality of sympathetic imagination—Henry James called it 'the civic use of the imagination'—must be an important aim in any form of education which is seeking the improvement and enrichment of the individual as a human being and as a social person. This is particularly true of secondary education for during this stage of their lives, most young people begin to question relationships, forms of

4

THE APPROACH TO HISTORY

behaviour and especially apparent inconsistencies of behaviour in other people in a more conscious way than they have done previously. They are eager to discuss the 'whys' of behaviour and to consider questions of value provided that these have a concrete setting which they can recognize. There is much within the subject matter of history about which this kind of thinking and discussion can take place and through which boys and girls can be helped to extend their experience of people. It has been largely with this particular aim in view that the so-called 'patch' approach to history —or the intensive study of all aspects of a short period—has been developed.

History, however, offers far more than this. Besides being concerned with individuals, it is also concerned with change and development, with man in relation to his environment and with his struggle to control and extend that environment. One important benefit of a study of history is that it offers an opportunity to deepen an understanding of the nature of change and development and a recognition of the common concern of humanity. This understanding of development and growth and the recognition of our own antecedents forms an essential part of human activity and seems to satisfy some basic need within men. A man gets a feeling of benefit and security when he discovers that someone else has had a similar experience to his own or has faced a similar problem to the one he is facing. History is a study which is especially suited to help for it allows men to form an attachment to the collective concerns of humanity, particularly in that it enables them to link themselves with the past and to come to an understanding of their origins and development so far. Even in quite young children this need is evident for often from about the age of 4 or 5 they ask all the questions about 'Where did I come from?', 'How did you get me?', 'What was I like when I was very small?' and 'What will I be like when I grow up?' These seem to be the beginnings of what may be called the historical impulse and represent a dawning recognition of change, growth and development, at first in a personal context. It is interesting to remember in this connection that the equivalent of history in primitive societies was usually the construction of a genealogy, often partly mythical, for the tribe or at least for its chief. The encouragement of a recognition of the continuity of human concern and values, of belonging to a community faced with similar problems and difficulties, each tackling them with the resources available at the time and on the whole searching for improvement through their struggles, these are central to a teacher's concern of helping a child to come to know more of himself and of the world.

Another important contribution which history can make to the education of children in the secondary school is that aspects of it can reinforce and extend their experience and understanding of the factors which make for successful living in a community. Learning to be a member of a community, to recognize the responsibilities and commitments which this involves and the benefits which can derive from such participation is chiefly done within the total context of the school by encouraging children to be conscious of the values for which the school stands and by providing a sound experience of being a member of a community. It is from this kind of experience, extending their experience of sharing in the family in their play, that their first notions of a need for regulations, and for them to subordinate at times their own inclinations to those of the group, comes. And it is from their understanding of the principles on which the communities of which they are real members exist that they derive the means to extend their understanding to take in such notions as justice and law, forms of government, citizenship, collective security, international co-operation. And it is in this extension of the understanding of the principles and purposes of community organization and life that a study of history can make yet another contribution which should form an important part of an education which is relevant both to the world we live in and to the needs and interests of children in secondary schools.

History can serve as a way of helping and encouraging children to think critically and independently, to learn to weigh evidence and to be discriminating in their approach to that evidence. Information which they can discover for themselves is likely to have much more significance for them than that which is too easily provided. The nature and possible point of view of the source of the evidence can be examined. If this is to happen, it is necessary that the pupils should have access to a different source of information so that their respective values and biases can be discussed. If the only source of information available to them is a textbook, pupils eventually come to think of history itself as something which exists mainly—or even only—in books. Moreover, any discussions about the relative value of evidence of different kinds tend to become academic exercises in which many of the children with whom this book is concerned do

6

not take an active part. On the other hand, a wide variety of sources of different kinds to which children have access can make this a valuable activity, and they can quickly become aware of the existence of different points of view and come to appreciate the need for a critical appraisal of evidence in the light of the source from which it comes.

There are, then, four main ways in which the study of history can contribute to a general education appropriate to the needs of pupils of average and less than average ability in the secondary schools. First, it can encourage the development of that aspect of the imagination by which we understand other people and it should provide an important part of the means whereby the experience and understanding of other people is extended beyond the limitations of immediate contacts. Secondly, it can offer to young people an opportunity to deepen their understanding of the nature of growth, change and development and in this way reinforce a recognition of the collective experience of humanity. Thirdly, it can be the means to enable young people to extend and deepen their understanding of the nature of social life and the factors which govern social life— the responsibilities of individuals to society and the recognition that the possession of rights implies the fulfilment of duties. Finally, it can contribute to the development of the powers of selection, interpretation, critical appraisal and judgement of evidence or information. The study of history at this level can offer these values; whether it does so depends upon the kind of approaches and material employed.

When deciding what material he will choose and what periods or topics he will select for study the history teacher is given a far greater degree of liberty by the structure of his subject than are teachers of many other school subjects. In most subjects there are certain elements which have to be studied and understood before other topics can be approached; this is true of mathematics which is strictly progressive in this sense or of foreign languages where the more common words and usages are studied before the less usual and more complicated formations. With subjects such as these the structure of the subject itself broadly dictates a pattern which the syllabus must follow. History is not a progressive subject in this sense, consequently the syllabuses used in secondary schools tend to vary widely.

Of the three main approaches to syllabus construction found in

7

the schools—the chronological, line of development and patch approaches—the most usual is still the chronological. This is the traditional approach and there is an obvious logic to studying the beginning of a story before looking at its ending. If it is the function of the history course to tell the story of the development of our civilization, then the chronological approach may be the most suitable. It will follow that the more junior pupils will study periods most remote in time and that senior pupils will be concerned with periods nearer to the present day. In order to operate such a syllabus, the more difficult aspects of earlier periods are usually excluded since they are obviously unsuited to younger pupils.

Critics of this approach claim that it requires pupils to learn about a varied mixture of happenings simply because they happen to occur during a particular period of time with the consequence that history lessons tend to become occasions for cramming the memory rather than opportunities for studying a 'well-knit sequence of elements'. It is also argued that where the teacher is making a general survey of a period, it is simply not possible to exclude completely all material unsuited to the stage of development of the pupils. Again if the aim of the history teacher is to teach a body of fact which is to be remembered, to teach the story of the development of our civilization, the sheer inability of the vast majority of children to carry forward this mass of unexercized fact from one year to another must cast serious doubt upon the value of this approach—certainly in the case of all except the brightest.

In an effort to overcome some of these drawbacks, some secondary schools have adopted the line of development approach to syllabus construction, the foremost advocate of which has been Professor M. V. C. Jeffreys. The influence of this approach may be seen in some of the syllabuses issued by the C.S.E. Boards. The Metropolitan Regional Board suggests in its regulations for 1969 a list of topics for candidates which includes the history of nursing, the history of costume, the history of transport and the history of government. It was stated by Jeffreys in his *History in Schools: The Study of Development* that such a line of development might supply 'a central theme from which subsidiary investigations can radiate as far as time and the pupils' intelligence allow'. He pointed out that the history of the alphabet could be studied in such a way as to show the importance of the Hebrews in the ancient world or the contribution of Greek to Roman culture.

A syllabus drawn up in this way certainly permits much greater flexibility and variation in the content of the work and where it is desirable to restrict the scope and to emphasize points likely to arouse more interest in teaching the less able, the advantage offered by this flexibility is considerable. Moreover a careful choice of topic can give pupils a much greater sense of purpose in studying than often arises from outline study of a period. One of the principal drawbacks which some teachers have found in practice has been the difficulty of effecting a proper inter-relation of the lines of development studied. It is too easy for pupils to study trade, agriculture and government in Ancient Greece in successive years as part of three separate lines of development without ever succeeding in bringing them together to form a comprehensive picture of life in Greece.

Since the Second World War the patch approach, as it is often described, has become fairly common. This involves abandoning largely the element of continuity and turning instead to the intensive study of limited and usually unrelated periods, for example Norman England or the age of Cromwell. The aim of those who follow this approach is to involve their pupils as thoroughly as possible in the imaginative experience of entering into another age with its different ways of thought and its different values, in this fashion to widen their outlook by giving them a thorough understanding of a period with a way of life which contrasts strongly with their own. Some of the advocates of this approach would claim that a weakness of the chronological and line of development systems is that since they are evolutionary, they tend to look at what is important today— parliamentary government or public health or transport—and to carry these current evaluations of significance into the past; the outcome of this being to judge other ages by standards and values which were not theirs.

Immersion in a small number of unrelated short periods or 'patches' naturally appears to be a totally inadequate arrangement to many of those who accept the need for children to be given some idea of their heritage, and some measure of understanding of the evolution and development of their present environment. A number of schools in which the patch approach has been employed do, in fact, tend to acknowledge the need to set the periods for intensive study in a wider historical perspective by undertaking brief outline courses which link the periods and by taking the chosen periods themselves in chronological order.

B

The syllabus chosen has to meet the requirements of the pupils and of the subject. The variety of practice existing in the schools suggests that the structure of the subject is in fact as well as in theory such as to permit the history teacher to exercise an unusual degree of flexibility in meeting the needs of his pupils. Thus, in order to determine his approach and material, the teacher must look pretty hard at the pupils themselves; it is not enough merely to think carefully about what he would like them to derive from their work in history, he must also consider what they can best study in terms of the stage of development of their capacities and experience. These must be the determining factors in selecting the best approach and the most suitable material to form the basis for a worthwhile history course.

This is a very large question and one on which, in so far as it is applied to fields of learning like history, little research work has been done. There are, however, a number of points which experience indicates may be stated with a fair degree of assurance. In the first place it is not simply the acquisition of information which makes for learning for in the words of A. N. Whitehead 'A merely well-informed man is the most useless man on God's earth'. Learning has to do not so much with knowing as with discovering, not so much with receiving ideas as with using and developing them. It is through exploration, through finding out for oneself and through reorganizing the ideas which arise from the experiences we have into fresh combinations that the growth and development recognized as learning takes place. The building up of the ideas by which children understand the world they live in is an active process which teachers can help, encourage and stimulate but not force or direct without running the risk of stopping it from happening altogether. This is true of the development of scientific and mathematical ideas and it is equally true of the development of the ideas which enable men to understand one another and the working of the communities in which they live.

One of the elements which is present in all worthwhile learning is a quality of absorption and of interest on the part of the person involved. Those activities which contribute significantly to a person's development are those which arouse a sense of wonder and commitment on his part. Activities prompted by genuine interest are characterized by a spontaneity and sense of timelessness, and while it is difficult to define closely what interest is, there are one or two points which are important which can be said about it.

10

1. People do not all become interested in the same things. Because they are individuals with different backgrounds and different levels of experience, their attention can be attracted by different aspects of the situations in which they find themselves. This is, of course, true for any class of children, the older they are the more diversified their interests tend to become. Therefore, in planning his course the history teacher will allow as much latitude as possible for children to have some choice within their work if interest is to have a chance to develop fully.

2. Interest is often caught in the company of other people—the real enthusiast can have a very infectious effect—and to overlook the importance and value of this frequent source of interest would be to ignore one of the most useful devices in education. In order to ensure that the enthusiasm is brought to the classroom it is very important that a teacher should not have to work to a syllabus which does not allow him enough opportunity to share his own interests and enthusiasms with his pupils. If he is to infect them with this wonder, he will achieve more when he is making contact with them through something that matters to him.

3. It should, perhaps, be added that there is no guaranteed way of always being able to rouse this quality of interest and absorption. Just to provide situations and experiences for a group of children which seem exciting does not necessarily mean that all of them will find something within it which will arouse their interest and concern. There are many possible reasons why some of them would find no stimulation in such a situation. It may be that they are already concerned with something else and that this overlays their receptivity to the new situation. Or it may be that because of previous difficulties and failures, they have temporarily lost the capacity to be interested and it will need carefully and patiently nurturing back to life.

Interest is one of the main factors in education since it is the *source* of effort and gives effort its value. One of the major criteria for selecting a course in history must be the likelihood of its engaging the interest and concern of the pupils for whom it is designed.

Another important consideration is that the sort of material forming the chosen course which the pupils are expected to work on should be within their capacity to understand and to think about in terms which are meaningful to them. The factors which determine at any given time the child's capacity to understand are the extent to which his thought patterns have developed, i.e. the maturation of his thinking abilities, and the nature and extent of his previous experiences and learning. It is factors such as these which determine whether or not a particular child at a particular time is really able to understand ideas like democracy, liberalism, nationalism and a balance of power. A great deal remains to be done to try to discover how a child's power to formulate ideas within this field takes place; more has been found out about the development of mathematical and scientific concepts. But such work as has been done suggests that the thought of the child of average ability will remain at the concrete, operational stage up to the age of 16 or so and the history course must be organized to take account of this. It is useless to present abstract material to pupils before they are ready to assimilate it. Indeed, there is some evidence to support the view that concepts which are introduced too soon or which are introduced in a situation too far removed from the pupil's experiences may well not only delay the time at which a fuller understanding can be reached but may prevent this from developing at all. Thus it is important to ensure that within a history course pupils should not be expected to undertake work which is too far beyond the frontiers of their earlier experience and learning.

A final factor which needs to be taken into account when deciding the nature of a course is the recognition that learning is an active process of exploration, discovery and experiment with ideas leading to some form of communication. Thus the course should contain the possibilities for pupils to search for evidence, to discover meaning and significance for themselves, to formulate simple hypotheses and to test them against evidence.

It is apparent, then, that there can be no simple answer to the question 'What history should secondary pupils of average and less than average ability study?' The correct answer in each situation must depend upon an assessment of the factors outlined here. There is undoubtedly a place for the study of earlier periods as well as recent or contemporary history and there are circumstances in which courses built on local history are as valuable as world history. It is almost certainly always wrong to claim that some series of events or some portion of history is so important that 'everyone must learn something about it'. To attempt to insist that everyone should take a particular course at some stage proved in past years to be wrong and ineffective when children of no great ability were compelled to learn chunks of political and constitutional history which they could not begin to comprehend; it would be no less wrong and equally futile to submit similar children today to courses consisting of 'things we all ought to know' about modern China or India unless such courses can be linked to and built upon the children's own experiences. The careful drawing of syllabuses and planning of courses must, moreover, be supported by a wise selection of suitable material and the employment of apt techniques.

2. The Contemporary World

The criteria outlined above seem to suggest that there is a strong case for regarding the field of contemporary history as a fruitful one from which to select. In the first place there is the availability of evidence in an abundance of forms to which boys and girls can have easy access. Newspaper accounts, films, television and radio programmes all serve to bring home to young people the history that is happening around them. Moreover, and perhaps most important of all, there are men and women who they can talk to who have lived through recent events and who can give first-hand accounts of the ways in which these affected them.

Contemporary history also gives a good opportunity to engage their interests since many of these centre on the world as it is and their concern can more easily be aroused. One consequence of the development of mass media is that people are conscious of living in an exciting period of world development, and the events which are taking place in many fields are the focus of many of the interests of the older children in secondary schools. This interest, duly encouraged, can become a powerful ally of the history teacher; it can also, of course, be easily squashed if their curiosity is not given the means and the encouragement to satisfy itself.

In addition, the rapidity of the pace of change and development in recent times makes it possible to illuminate the nature of change and growth, and the dependence of the next step on what has gone before, without having to make a possibly superficial study of a long period of time.

Like any other period, contemporary history also presents its particular problems in the classroom. One of the most obvious is that of interpretation. History teachers are well aware of the difficulties that can arise in handling controversial material. The question of avoiding bias and of not giving false impressions is one which those dwell upon who feel that contemporary history has no place in schools. This difficulty can take various forms; occasionally it may be impossible with the best will on the part of the teacher to arrive at the truth of a controversial situation in which he is caught

14

up along with other members of the community. In these circumstances it may be argued that the passage of time alone can enable a more dispassionate approach to the truth. This may be so, but the absence of a currently controversial issue from the school syllabus will not protect the pupils from currently prejudiced thinking on a topic, while it is always possible that discussion of the matter in class may encourage a more critical attitude.

Another fear sometimes experienced is that the less able children are unable to distinguish bias and prejudice, but some teachers of children of limited ability have found that they are quite capable of sorting a lot of this out for themselves provided that it is handled honestly. The idea of a difference of point of view is one that makes sense to them, and which they can develop a healthy attitude towards, provided that it is introduced to them in a tangible way and from examples which are within, or are relatable to, their own experiences. One of the main differences between the academically able and the less able is not so much that the former can apprehend ideas which the latter cannot approach but that they can make the abstraction from example to idea more readily and quickly. The less able can often cope with ideas provided that these ideas are recognizable within concrete situations with which they come to terms through their own experiences in the first instance. This is what a study of contemporary history can offer to the young people for it has as its source material living men whom they can encounter, films they can see, newspapers they can read and places they can visit.

The increasing appeal in the schools of twentieth-century history can be seen in the syllabuses which have been issued by the new regional boards conducting the C.S.E. examinations. Many of the pupils with whom this book is concerned will never prepare for any public examinations, but these published syllabuses and those followed by pupils who are not publicly examined are often similar in outline even if they are modified to meet different aptitudes and abilities. Many, but not all, of the new examining boards have attempted to offer teachers a very wide choice of periods for study but, even so, there is a distinct emphasis in the overall picture on recent history and, to some extent, on social and economic history. The Yorkshire Regional Board for instance in its scheme for 1969 states that it puts forward only three syllabuses—in Civics, social and economic history of Great Britain since 1700 and modern world history—because these modern topics are most evidently in demand.

It adds that: 'The History Panel thought it might be an advantage to teachers if its motives in selecting these syllabuses were made clear in an introduction to each syllabus. The Panel recognizes that some reasons can be brought to bear for teaching almost any topic or period in History in particular circumstances. It supports the view that the 16-year-old pupil, often a school leaver, should be able to see the relevance of history to his own life and to the circumstances of our own time. Therefore all its plans envisage a continuation of the study into the Present.' Much the same argument is advanced by the North Regional Board: 'This syllabus assumes that the history which today's pupils need is the history of their own world in recent times. It should show them how this world has developed and should attempt to explain it as it is today. It aims to educate future citizens of this democracy in a deeper and wider understanding so that they will prove worthy and responsible citizens of a wider world.'

Probably most schools still follow a broadly chronological approach in their history teaching, consequently the contemporary or near contemporary work tends to fall in the fourth or fifth year. This is the current position in a large comprehensive school where many of the ideas discussed are being put into practice. This school has 1900 boys and girls, from 11 to 18 years of age, drawn from a very mixed social background varying from a mining district to residential villages housing commuting residents who go to work in a large city near by. All pupils take history for the first three years and have six to eight periods for this subject in a ten-day timetable. In the fourth and subsequent years history is studied by those wishing to take it in the G.C.E. and the C.S.E. All of those who are not aiming at a public examination study history as part of their programme during their last year at school.

There are good modern facilities with five history rooms, three being grouped together in one part of the school and two in another. The equipment available includes such aids as a film strip projector, tape recorder and a 16 mm. projector. Books are divided between the two bases and are drawn from stock as required, there is also a supply of tape recordings of suitable broadcast programmes, film strips, wall charts, records, models and modelling materials. The aim is always to make use of as wide a variety of material as possible. One syllabus is used for the whole range of ability. With a careful choice of topics from the syllabus it has been found that boys and girls of rather less than average ability can develop their judgement and discrimination through the discussion of material and the pursuit of simple tasks. This is seen as being well worth while if only to enable them to stand up more successfully to the increasing barrage of the 'hidden persuaders'.

The aims of history teaching in the school are seen as:

1. To help pupils to understand, at whatever level of comprehension is possible to them, some of the issues of our time.
2. To feel an awareness that the everyday things with which they are familiar result from a process of development. A knowledge of man's past achievements should produce a measure of humility and tolerance.
3. To reflect in the teaching the dictum of R. G. Collingwood that: 'To the boy or girl the activities whose history he or she is studying are not spectacles to be watched but experiences to be lived through.'
4. To help pupils appreciate that freedom and rights carry with them responsibilities and duties.

The syllabus followed in the school has a broad chronological framework from which topics suited to the age and ability of pupils are selected.

Outline of the Syllabus

FIRST YEAR

Term One   Personal, Family and Local history.
Today's world with its examples of variations in the pattern of development; e.g. contrast between Aborigines and Western Society.
Time chart to show the development of Ancient civilizations.
Major study—Ancient Greece.

Term Two   Rome and Roman Britain.

Term Three Saxons, Vikings and Normans.

SECOND YEAR

Term One   Portrait of an Age—The Middle Ages.

Term Two   The Era of the Renaissance.
The Days of Elizabeth I.

Term Three Civil War and Restoration.

THIRD YEAR

Term One   Empire to Commonwealth.

Term Two   The Changing Face of Britain.

Term Three The Rise of Modern World Powers.

FOURTH AND FIFTH YEARS

'O' Level Course: World Powers 1870–1939.
Democracy and Dictatorship 1870–1950.
Economic and Social History 1700–1950.

C.S.E. Courses: The Last Hundred Years in Britain.
World History 1900–1964.

Leavers' Course: Recent History and Civics—(as part of a 'Humanities' course).

Contemporary history is introduced in this scheme in the third year; this gives an opportunity to those pupils who will be dropping history after the third year—because they have chosen to take G.C.E. or C.S.E. in other subjects—to study the background to modern Britain, the Commonwealth and the Great Powers. In this way they can be given some knowledge of contemporary history on which to base their future understanding of the society in which they will live their lives. Candidates taking history as a public examination subject build on the work in third and subsequent years.

The general line of approach which has been found effective for the third year work is to discuss the current position and to see how it has arisen.

Empire to Commonwealth—Outline of the first term's work

A. *What is meant by the concept of Commonwealth:*
member nations:
purpose: functions: organization: advantages: problems:
Commonwealth conferences:
Rhodesia as a problem:

B. *Background to Empire:*
possessions in the early eighteenth century, how they had been acquired, attitude of the home government to them:
colonies in North America, conquest of Canada, discontent and

rebellion in American colonies, impact of the loss of the thirteen colonies:

position at the end of the eighteenth century, Canada, India, work of Cook, colonization of Australia, New Zealand:

C. *Empire in the mid-nineteenth century:*

developments in Canada, Australia and New Zealand:

Africa, Cape Colony, conflict with the Boers, foundation of the Boer States:

India, expansion of British rule, mutiny, 1858 Act:

'accidental' nature of the growth of many of these large colonies scattered across the world, Australia as a dumping ground for convicts, India from the trade of a great commercial company, etc:

D. *Growth of the Empire, 1858–1914:*

strengthening of ties, impact of emigration, government action, e.g. Disraeli and the Suez Canal:

development of self-government and the concept of dominion status, Canada, Australia and New Zealand:

pattern of change in Africa, conquest by European powers, exploration and development, e.g. Livingstone and Rhodes, Boer War and its sequel:

Far East, increase in interests of European countries:

E. *From Empire to Commonwealth:*

the Empire and the First World War, attitude of Canada, Australia, New Zealand, S. Africa:

representation at the Peace Conference:

1931 Statute of Westminster:

India's continuing struggle, personalities, success in 1947:

evolving pattern since Second World War in Africa, Asia and the West Indies.

The Changing Face of Britain—*Outline of the second term's work*

A. *The Position today:*

population, distribution, size:

occupations:

conditions of life, work, leisure, welfare:

communications:

19

B. *The Position in the early eighteenth century:*
   population, distribution, size:
   occupations:
   conditions of life, work, leisure, welfare:
   communications:

C. *The Changing pattern of agriculture and industry:*
   main features:
   reasons:
   consequences, wealth of the country, effect on lives of people:

D. *Towns and factories:*
   conditions, improvements and improvers:

E. *Changing political pattern:*
   chart to show main changes from eighteenth century to the present day:
   trade unions and co-operative societies:

F. *Changing pattern of society in the last 60 years:*
   Welfare State:
   continuing industrial revolution:
   health:
   housing:
   fashion:
   leisure:

Project work is well suited for dealing with much of this material and these topics are suggested for projects:

Improvers in Agriculture/Textiles/Iron and Steel/Communications
The Enclosure Movement
Coal 1760–1960
Housing development
Education
Conquest of Disease
Growth of Democracy
Reformers, e.g. Wilberforce, Fry, Howard, Peel
Recreation

Work undertaken with those boys and girls who are preparing for 'O' level of the G.C.E. in the fourth and fifth years is not immediately relevant here. In the case of those preparing for C.S.E. every effort is made to bring home to individuals the relevance of their work in history to their everyday lives. The courses themselves build upon the more recent sections of third year work. In order to get boys and girls to relate the developments they will study in history to their own lives and the lives of those with whom they have or have had personal contact—their parents, grandparents and great-grandparents—they each complete the following questionnaire at the beginning of the fourth year.

C.S.E. Course Questionnaire

Please try to complete this questionnaire with the help of your parents.

Father's name:
Date of birth: Place of birth:
Occupation:

Mother's name: Maiden name:
Date of birth: Place of birth:
Occupation before marriage:

Name of father's father:
Date of birth: Place of birth:
Occupation:

Name of father's mother: Maiden name:
Date of birth: Place of birth:
Occupation before marriage:

Name of mother's father:
Date of birth: Place of birth:
Occupation:

Name of mother's mother: Maiden name:
Date of birth: Place of birth:
Occupation before marriage:

Name of father's grandfather:
Date of birth: Place of birth:
Occupation:

Name of father's grandmother:
Date of birth: Place of birth:
Occupation before marriage:

Name of mother's grandfather:
Date of birth: Place of birth:
Occupation:

Name of mother's grandmother:
Date of birth: Place of birth:
Occupation before marriage:

By trying to find out the answers to these questions you will be taking part in a piece of research. The main purpose of this will be to demonstrate the contact between the present and the past. Any discussion of how things have changed, why they have changed and the consequences of change must involve reference to people and amongst these were your families, your forebears. About them we can ask the questions the answers to which give a picture of the changing pattern of society.

What work did they do?
How have wages changed?
What of housing conditions?
What about their recreation, fashions of dress, transport?

History tells us something of how we become what we are. It tells of changes which have benefited us. It has lessons to teach of how we can contribute in our turn to ensure the preservation of the best in our society and help to bring about change where this can be beneficial.

Here, as ever, aims and methods are closely related. The stimulation of interest and the desire to find out can be induced to feed itself to some extent provided the techniques employed go beyond chalk and talk. Accordingly, a great deal of the study for the C.S.E. is based upon reference books, pictures, local history records, eye-witness accounts, films and film strips, tape recordings and the like.

Boys and girls who are not preparing for any public examinations continue their work in history after the third year in the context of studies in the Humanities. The Humanities embrace English, History, Geography and Religious Education and form part of the course for the final year designed to equip pupils for the world beyond the school. Aspects of the Humanities with which the historian deals form a course in civics and recent history.

A. *The Pupil and the Community in which he lives*

    1. rates, income tax, welfare benefits and national insurance:

    2. local and central government—elections, right to vote and the history of the widening of the franchise, use of the right to vote: other systems of government:

    3. industrial relations—trade unions, employers, productivity and incomes, 'doing a fair day's work for a fair day's pay':

    4. law and order—treatment of crime, capital punishment, value of very long sentences, compensation for victims.

B. *Communications*

    the press, radio, television, books,

    organization of the newspaper industry, reduction in number of papers,

    historical growth of the right of free speech and of the press, attitude of newspapers, education, etc. under other forms of government.

C. *Foreign affairs and the world overseas*

    our relationships with other peoples, international trade,

    everyday necessities from overseas, reasons for taking an interest in other countries,

    Europe, Common Market issue, E.F.T.A., defence,

    unification of Germany, relations with Russia and Eastern Europe, the historical background to these issues,

    U.S.A., how and why it has come to occupy its present position,

    Africa, Asia and the underdeveloped countries,

    United Nations, purpose, background to some of the more pressing current problems which beset it e.g., Vietnam and China, Israel and the Arabs.

D. *Attitudes*

    on what are people's attitudes based?

    factors involved in the development of attitudes to such issues as world hunger, colour questions, Welfare State, care for the old and infirm, war, nuclear disarmament, etc.

    As an example of the way in which this material may be treated one might look more closely at some of the questions arising under the heading Law and Order (A4). Here it was possible to develop the issues of the apt punishment of crime and compensation for victims against a background of events of which the pupils already had some knowledge from the television and newspapers. The Great Train Robbery, the murder of a policeman, the Moors Murder Case, the murder of a young man trying to stop a thief and the recent Criminal Justice Bill were familiar to various members of the class and provided illustrative material. Some of the historical background to such issues came from a reading of an account of life in an early convict settlement and from Dickens's comments on a public execution. A tape recording of a broadcast on the plight of dependants added to the sense of urgency of the problems. Thus in these ways the pupils' own knowledge was raised to the full light of consciousness and added to; they were able to offer opinions and make judgements on the basis of the evidence surveyed.

The materials which have been most useful in teaching these boys and girls have been tape recordings of B.B.C. broadcasts for schools, film strips and the sort of background provided by the more stimulating television programmes; much that is useful as 'follow up' can often be found in newspaper articles and in the colour supplements. In teaching topics which arise out of the Humanities programme the aim is to try to assemble in work rooms selections of material, books, charts, strips and tapes not only of the history department but also from the geography and English stock. It is essential to have plenty of reference material readily available; it is also essential for the time-tabling to be designed to allow blocks of time for the introduction of a topic and its pursuit whether in discussion groups or project work, reading or movement out from the school to the field of inquiry—libraries, museums, old folks' homes, etc.

A great deal of value has arisen from some of these forms of contact with the community such as the visits of young people to old peoples' homes armed with a tape recorder and a questionnaire which has been composed as part of a project. The reminiscences gathered in this way prove to be useful and stimulating sources leading in to such matters as the General Strike, life in wartime conditions, the cost of living 50 years ago and changes in the value of money. Naturally one must accept that the passage of time blurs the memory and individual reminiscences may well not be accurate, but such material gathered from a number of old people tends to build up a broadly accurate picture with the odder tricks of individual memory being shown for what they are.

Another form of contact which has proved of value has been to invite certain people from outside the school to speak or to take part in a forum; J.P.s, welfare officers and probation officers among others have helped in this way. It has been found to be essential to give visitors clear advice on the age, ability and powers of concentration of the members of the group they will be meeting.

In these ways the teaching of contemporary history has been able to provide a bridge from the school to the community outside for boys and girls of very modest academic potential.

3. The Relevance of Earlier History

For the teacher engaged in syllabus-making, contemporary history has strong attractions, but it is extremely doubtful whether it should form the whole of a syllabus. There are other factors to be considered before the syllabus is finally made. The Schools Council Working Paper No. 2 *Raising the School-leaving Age* 1965 (paras. 46, 47, 48) makes some relevant points.

More is however at issue than simply relating the work of the schools to the pupils' own view of their needs, to their own central interests, and to their own evaluation of what is relevant. These are the points of departure, and at least half the task is that of finding starting points, methods of work, and materials for assisting the process of learning which, so to speak, come right home to the pupils. But the other half of the task is to carry the pupils forward, so that what is taught has relevance not only to the pupils' present condition, but also to at least the next stage in their future development and understanding.

The teacher must necessarily see more deeply than the pupil can, partly because he is older, better educated and longer experienced, but also because he is trustee for a social view of what is good and useful, the full implications of which lie far beyond the pupils' present experience. This experience may well give the pupils insights into the likely personal relevance of skills and certain other elements in the curriculum. But they will be left prisoners of their own experience if the teacher cannot find a way of so enlarging their vision and understanding that they come to see value for themselves in gaining some understanding of Man's total experience, and with it some capacity to contribute to its further enlargement.

Sound syllabus making must rest upon a consideration of the two factors of the nature of the subject and the nature of the pupils. 'I teach history' is not enough. Nor on the other hand is the cry of the child-centred educator 'I teach John'. Both must be considered. If it is accepted that the particular value of history in secondary schools is that it offers insights of depth and length of perspective which literature on the one hand and current affairs on the other, cannot give, then two implications follow for history in school. Firstly that some impression of the chronological structure of history must be given. This does not mean a narrative of history trying to give equal weight and time to everything that happened from the Greeks to Mao Tse-tung, taking five years of a school course. Rather it means outlines, and brief sketches of the main developments and landmarks, taking a few lessons of exposition and a generous use of time-charts. Secondly it implies that there must be a study of the past in some depth—in periods, or patches or eras—and these studies in depth can then be related to the general developments in the history of man.

A consideration of that other factor relevant to syllabus-making, namely the thinking abilities of our pupils, leads to similar conclusions. The basic abilities necessary for an understanding of history may be listed as follows:

i. the ability to classify objects (such as tools and weapons) and events (such as wars, accessions, birthdays, visits);

ii. the ability to appreciate the lengths of time intervals;

iii. the ability to order sequences on a time scale and to use chronological conventions of historians (such as B.C. and A.D.);

iv. the ability to recognize that disparate events occurred simultaneously;

v. the ability to understand that ways of life can be different;

vi. the ability to understand something of the problems and techniques of historical research, of how historians get to know, and of what constitutes historical evidence;

vii. the ability to follow a story, and see how its events are intelligible by reference to what has gone before;

viii. the ability to sympathize with human beings as they meet the contingencies of life;

ix. the ability to conceive possibilities—to consider not only the concrete, what is and what has been, but also what could have been and what can be;

x. the ability to understand concepts used frequently in history, either directly or by implication, such as *rule, authority, sovereignty, revolution, kingship, dictatorship.*

Of these various abilities, some, perhaps the first six listed, would be characteristic of that phase of intellectual development, known in

'Piagetian' terms as that of concrete operational thinking. The other abilities would be characteristic of the later stage of formal operational thought. Now most children, certainly of the average and below average ability levels, between the ages of 11 and 15 are still in the stage of concrete operational thinking. The real and the present are the data of their thought and such characteristics of mature historical thinking as the ability to make meaningful contrasts, to see events in perspective, to understand motives, to elucidate consequences, are still as yet in embryo. If this is accepted then the history syllabus in the early years of the secondary school should be giving to the pupils those experiences and activities from which the characteristics of mature historical thinking can emerge. First it should be providing constant references to the passage of time, perhaps by Lines of Development work, by using and making time-charts, and by the experience of stories or the study of *patches* in a chronological sequence rather than in a higgledy-piggledy order. Secondly, there should be study of what is real and concrete to the child, that is the study of the present and recent events, in father's or grandfather's time. This may involve putting some contemporary history earlier in the school course than is usual, but if by harnessing the pupil's concern with his present world, it can further the eventual maturity of his thought, then this is to be welcomed. Thirdly it should offer some studies in depth, either in a *patch* of history or a topic investigated as a *line of development*. Fourthly it should ensure that concepts commonly encountered in history such as *kingship* and *rule, war* and *revolution* are discussed. Fifthly it should consider the value of evidence in history and the question of 'How do we know?' Finally it should present history as a story, having a beginning, a middle and an end.

If the syllabus and teaching of the earlier years of a secondary school course, say up to the age of 14 or 15, fulfils these conditions then in the later years pupils can come to grips with *real* history that is an attempt to re-create the life of a community in the past, in depth and with accuracy. This would involve the study of a period of history earlier than that of recent times. Such a study could be part of a Humanities course for school leavers. It would have a purpose for the pupil quite different from that given by the course in Civics and Recent History outlined in the previous chapter, but nevertheless it would be equally worthwhile. The contention here is that recent history should not replace the history of earlier periods, but that both are desirable for the secondary school child, the one by contrast illuminating the other. Alternatively this study of an earlier period in depth could be that chosen for the C.S.E. or G.C.E. examination. Certainly whether an early or modern period as a topic is chosen for the examination course, that it should be a study in depth rather than a long outline course seems most desirable from all points of view, the pupil's, the teacher's and even the examiner's. A study in depth more easily engages the interests, and is more readily comprehensible, while at the same time it would seem the natural culmination of that practice of historical skills which has been experienced in the earlier years of the secondary school and which can now be used to effect in the study of the life of specific communities in the past.

The specimen history syllabus below reflects these various considerations; chronological outlines, the value of considering at an early stage the present and the concrete, and the importance of studies in depth.

A Possible Five-year Secondary School History Syllabus

FIRST YEAR

Lines of Development: Homes, Transport, Health, Food and Agriculture.

SECOND YEAR

Term One   Environmental Study and Local History.

Term Two   Ancient civilizations, with emphasis on Egypt and Greece.

Term Three Rome and Roman Britain.

THIRD YEAR

Term One
Term Two } Middle Ages 450–1485.

Term Three Reformation and Revolution (aspects of sixteenth- and seventeenth-century history).

FOURTH YEAR

Term One
Term Two } The Modern World. Ideally as part of a syllabus in which history is integrated with other subjects
Term Three } such as geography and literature.

29

FIFTH YEAR

For examination candidates:

Choice of whatever period one can enthuse about for C.S.E. or G.C.E. examinations. It does not have to be the modern period.

For non-examinees:

1. Lines of Development on Government, or Crime and Punishment, for example.
2. A 'Patch' or 'Patches'.

Both of these would be seen as particular contributions which history could make to a 'Humanities' Synthesis.

So far it has been argued both from considerations of the nature of history as a discipline and from what is known of the thinking abilities of the pupils in question, that contemporary history alone is not enough. The advantage of choosing an earlier period of history for the less able child may be seen by considering the medieval period.

The first advantage is that the medieval period offers an excellent field for meaningful contrast with our present environment and times. The medieval agricultural economy can be contrasted either with the present-day industrial economy in Britain or with another agricultural economy in some part of the present world, perhaps in Africa. An age in which Church influence dominated can be contrasted with an age when the Churches are divided and largely ignored by society. A period when England underwent conquest can be contrasted with a period when it escaped it. An age when parliament had its origin can be contrasted with an age when parliament, or as some might assert, when its prime minister, dominates politics. An age when the average expectation of life was 28 years can be contrasted with an age when most may expect to reach the psalmist's 'three score years and ten'. A period of little material comfort can be opposed to an age of general material ease.

Secondly, the medieval period has the attraction of being a past age, wholly different from the present and this together with its remoteness appeals to many pupils. Knights and all the paraphernalia of chivalry, monks, friars and pilgrims, manorial life, merchants and craftsmen and their gilds, wars and weapons, rulers and revolts, all this exerts a fascination for these children. Romantic though it may be, it is not to be despised for it provides that initial source of interest in a subject which the teacher can use and mould. Even if in the beginning distance adds enchantment to the pupil's view of the middle ages, as his or her study deepens a more realistic, a more historical view will replace it. If many pupils feel the pull of a past which is wholly different from their present then a history syllabus which recognizes this is at least assured of some interested response from its pupils. It will avoid too that jaded apathy towards history characteristic of many secondary school children in their last years at school to which one young pupil doing 'O' level modern history gave articulation when she said 'It is like reading a lot of out-of-date newspapers'.

Thirdly, the medieval period is in some ways a less complicated period of history than contemporary history, or at least it can be taught as such at school level without great distortion. For example, the pattern of life is slower, the changes in society appear less vigorous when compared with those which have taken place since the invention of the internal combustion engine.

Fourthly, for those who see value in history only in as much as it explains the development of the present, the medieval period is essential. Here may be found the origins of those forces and institutions which continue to shape the present: the forces of capitalism and nationalism, the institutions of parliament, the law courts and the universities.

Similarly, for the supporters of world history the medieval period has its attractions, for it was a fully cosmopolitan period. Certainly it is quite unhistorical to study England in the middle ages as an entity in itself. It was subject to barbarian invasions which had their origins in Mongolia. It was part of a much wider Christendom and Christendom was partly in conflict, partly in relationship with the world of Islam and the East. The Anglo-Norman knight, crusading in the Holy Land, had origins which were far from native. They began with a technical invention of the Chinese, namely the stirrup, which slowly found its way to the West and made possible that most effective military force of the middle ages, the knight-on-horseback. The knight brought the Carolingians and the Normans to power, and feudalism to fruition and on the way England was absorbed into a world stretching far beyond its island shores. Crusaders, traders, scholars and missionaries linked West and East, and from the beginning of the thirteenth century fears and rumours of Genghis Khan and the Mongols ensured that these links, however tenuous, continued.

Stories are the essence of history and they remain a vital attraction for all secondary school children regardless of their ability. The middle ages has its full share of them. Stories of King Arthur were 'best sellers' throughout the medieval period, and their magic continues to entrance young, and even old, today. The James Bond of his age, King Arthur can arouse the interest of school children as much as James Bond himself and the comparisons that can be made between the two, and the differing myths and values that surround them are as significant and worth while as the stories themselves. Gregory the Great, Bede, Offa, Boniface, Charlemagne, Alfred, William the Conqueror, Hereward, Ailred of Rievaulx, Frederick Barbarossa, Henry II and Becket, Richard the Lion Heart, King John, St. Francis—the list could be extended, and the teacher can make his own choice.

The medieval period also offers scope for a variety of approach and for practical work which few other periods can equal. Medieval historical sites, churches, monasteries and castles are legion in this country and offer obvious opportunities for out-of-school visits and field-work. Alternatively within the four walls of a classroom medieval life can be resurrected easily and inexpensively. Villages, three-field systems and castles can all be modelled out of simple materials such as cardboard, clay, glue and paints. In making models some pupils can experience an earlier period of history such as medieval life more directly than they can some later periods. The individual pupil can make a pot much as a medieval man would have made one, but he can in no way make a pot as Wedgwood did. The medieval period also offers heraldry, a subject which either explicitly or implicitly illustrates so much of medieval life and with opportunities for practical and imaginative work which the less able child can manage.

Finally, a study of the middle ages offers an experience of different values to consider and measure against those relevant and prevalent in the contemporary world. The effect should be to make a girl or boy a questioner, a doubter and a critic of his own life, his times and the actions and public professions of others. Moreover, and this is equally important, it should make him or her a realistic and not a romantic, head-in-the-clouds critic. In the context of the average school child this means that he will question what his teachers, newspapers, radio, television and prime minister might tell him.

PLATE I

Making the soups and flavourings

Beating the meat to make it tender

Trapping Birds.

Making Butter

PLATE I and PLATE II (over page): Examples of children's work (*see page* 74)

PLATE IV

(20 Child	Villein's Child	Lord's Child
Gets up at	Gets up at	Gets up at
Breakfast at	Breakfast at	Breakfast at
Lunch at		
Supper (tea)	Supper at	Supper at
Bed at	Bed at	Bed at
(20 Man	Villein	Lord
(20 Woman	Villein's Wife	Lord's Wife

PLATE IV: A comparison between our lives and those of medieval folk (*see page* 56)

A Suggested Syllabus on the Middle Ages for 13-14-year-olds

Introduction and explanation of middle ages 450-1450
   Outline of the period seen as Christendom though with particular
   reference to English History and the theme of the growth of the
   English nation.

Barbarian invasions, East to West
Invasions of Anglo-Saxons in Britain
King Arthur—fact and fiction
   (This particular theme can be used both for its engaging interest
   and as a focal point of much medieval history—its Christian faith,
   chivalry, nationalism, etc.)

St. Augustine and Christian Missions, emphasizing two-way traffic
   of English missions to Europe.
Charlemagne
Unification of England: Ethelbert to Alfred
Anglo-Saxon ways of life
The Norman Conquest

Law and Order—the growth of Central Government and its clash
   with 1. The Church—Becket and 2. The Nobles—King John to
   the Wars of the Roses.
Life on the Manor
Church Life and Architecture
The Crusades
Edward I
Hundred Years War
Development of English Language
Chaucer—can be used as a focus to draw various themes of medieval
   life together.

Themes to be taken up as group or individual activities include: The
   Manor, Work and Play; Monastic Life; Development of the Castle;
   A Pilgrimage; Knights, Warfare, Arms and Heraldry; Home Life;
   Clothes, Furniture, Food and Drink; Trade and Transport.

Biographical lessons might include: Gregory the Great, Bede, Offa,
   Boniface, Charlemagne, Henry I (the Fowler), William the
   Conqueror, Hereward, Gregory VII, Roger of Salisbury, Ailred of
   Rievaulx, Henry II, Becket, Frederick Barbarossa, Richard the
   Lion Heart, William Marshall, King John, St. Louis IX, St.
   Francis, Frederick II, Simon de Montfort, Robert Bruce, The Black
   Prince, Henry V, Joan of Arc, Richard III.

4. The Place and Value of Local History

For more than half a century the value of local history in schools has been acknowledged. Numerous books and articles have recommended that it should be taught, though there have been considerable differences of opinion about both the reasons for and the extent of its inclusion in school history syllabuses. The debate on this continues and each individual teacher will decide for himself the validity or otherwise of the various arguments which are advanced for the study of local history in schools.

First, and most common, it is argued that local history is of value as the handmaid of national or general history; it illustrates and makes vivid and concrete the generalized assertions and explanations of the historian. In 1908 when the Board of Education in its circular on the teaching of history in secondary schools, proclaimed that 'it is essential that in each school attention should be paid to the history of the town and district in which it is situated', it had this very reason in mind for it continued that teachers should make 'constant reference to the history of the locality as illustrative of the general history'. This same argument has been restated many times since then, often with its corollary that through local history the actual experience and present environment of pupils can be related to wider themes and consequently history becomes a far more interesting, relevant and memorable subject in the curriculum. Always, however, proponents of this argument have been concerned to assert that local history should not be a narrow parochial study but should serve the larger purpose of forwarding a more general historical knowledge. One of the first books which gave a detailed analysis of the place of local history in schools, *History Teaching for Today* published in 1935, by Eric C. Walker, made this point quite specifically.

> Too often Local History is considered as an incidental attraction, if not as an actual sop: it is the sugar on the unpalatable but necessary pill that has to be administered to the young. This point of view has tended to create in the child's mind an impression that Local History is 'good fun' which can have no true relation with the conventional lesson 'on the syllabus'. If, on the other hand, one

starts from local conditions and, where necessary, works outward, the child's interest is captured and the sublimation of parochial to the justly weighed and finely balanced national or international point of view is attained without hiatus or ellipsis.

Secondly, it is argued that local history is a most effective way of showing pupils what history is and how it is made, and of giving them some acquaintance with the sources and research methods of history. Pupils can be shown how recent research by historians in the localities has enabled them to present a more accurate account of historical changes on a national scale. For example general accounts of the enclosure movement in the Tudor period rely heavily upon researches made in smaller, more local areas. Like the scientist who studies natural phenomena with the aid of a microscope, so the historian uses local history to focus on small units of history in order either to substantiate or to question general theories about the nature of historical change. In addition to this, local history can also give pupils a more direct experience of how history is made. For in local study they can see and handle the actual sources of history, whether they be documentary or material. They can use them to construct their own histories and so obtain some experience of 'finding out' which differs only in degree and not in kind from the historical research of the professional historian.

A third and more recent view of the place and value of local history has a quite different point of departure. It claims that local history and national history are two different studies. Local history is not just part of national history but deserves to be studied for its own sake. A group of historians emanating from the University of Leicester and led by H. P. R. Finberg and W. G. Hoskins have been the most constant proponents of this view. Far from studying local areas in the hope of combining them to make a truer picture of the nation, they urge the study of local communities which so often have a life of their own quite different from that of neighbouring communities and have local loyalties far more real and compelling than those occasionally owed to the national community. This view has its advocates in schools. Like world history, it provides a corrective to the impression which may so often be gained from school syllabuses, that the nation is and always has been the main factor in human affairs. It also provides a study in the history of the local community for its own sake and in depth 'because it was there'.

Fourthly, arguments for the inclusion of local history in the school curriculum are advanced on psychological and sociological grounds. Each child, it is asserted, needs to belong to or have roots in a society which nurtures him and which 'makes sense' for him. If the units of this society are too large he will feel insecure and as a consequence both his growth as a person and as a member of a community with a sense of social responsibility, will be hindered. The historical understanding of the environment, the feeling that they belong to a pattern of life which was there before they were and which surrounds them in their childhood with order and stability, is therefore a necessary part of children's educational experience. The home and the family will help to provide this but in the present age of social mobility when families are uprooted and scattered and new communities mushroom into existence almost overnight, the study of local history in school becomes a valuable means to the creation of personal security and social responsibility.

In deciding what part local history should play in a school syllabus individual teachers will place varying emphasis on the values of local history outlined above. Usually local history emerges in the syllabus in three main ways. It may be a constant factor used whenever possible to arouse and sustain interest and to illustrate general themes. Or it may be studied as a *patch* of local history giving to the pupils all the advantages of study in depth including the use of the various skills of *finding out*. Or local history may be included as part of an environmental study in which work in history, geography and science is combined.

In the teaching of the less able children in schools, local history is particularly valuable. So often for them, history seems remote. It is a string of facts in a book which carry little or no conviction. Local history can, however, make concrete what is general and remote by introducing detail which is the more convincing since it includes the name of places which pupils know. For example, the normal school syllabus, textbook and lesson dealing with British history in the eighteenth century is sure to mention John Wilkes and his various struggles for political liberties. It is not easy, however, to convey to pupils that in his time Wilkes had an importance which went far beyond the confines of Middlesex and London. Only when illustrations from local historical sources are used to reinforce the general accounts does John Wilkes begin to take on some meaning as a 'friend to Liberty' who really mattered. For pupils in the West

Riding of Yorkshire the following two extracts from the *Leeds Mercury* have an obvious relevance though even for pupils in other parts of the country they would be useful in showing the extent of Wilkes's influence and his national importance.

Leeds Mercury, Tuesday, April 24, 1770

At Bradford, the morning (Wednesday previous) was ushered in with ringing of bells, which continued till ten at night, and in the evening were illuminations, and the following, we hear, was given at the sole expence of Mr. Richard Shackleton, at the Bull's Head, viz. A bonfire of 45 load of coals; a curious representation of the figures 45, composed of 45 candles, under which was wrote, in large characters, WILKES AT LIBERTY: also a supper to the sons of liberty, which consisted of 45 lbs. of roast beef; legs of mutton and tongues 45 lb.; three hams 45 lb.; 45 fowls; a lamb 45 lbs.; 45 lb. of bread; 45 lb. of vegetables; 45 gallons of ale and 45 bowls of punch; after supper all the loyal healths were drunk.

We hear from Wakefield, Halifax, Doncaster, Sheffield, and most of the towns in the West Riding, that they had likewise great rejoicings on Wednesday last. At Leeds there were bonfires, and some windows illuminated with exactly 45 candles; at one house, in particular, where several friends were assembled to sup and spend the evening, a curious candlestick, holding 45 lights, was constructed, which had a very agreeable appearance, and at the foot of it the following was printed:

> In Honour of John Wilkes, Esq.
> I really wish that Man may thrive
> That drinks a Health to Forty-Five.

After supper many loyal and constitutional toasts were drunk; and the company, who stile themselves *The Patriotic Society*, agreed to meet on the 18th of April annually, in order to commemorate that ever-memorable day.

Leeds Mercury, Tuesday, August 21, 1770

'On Friday a Travelling Gentleman (who had a small cast with one of his eyes), stopping at the Old King's Arms in this town, it was directly rumoured that Mr. Wilkes was come: which soon brought together a great crowd of people, who were confirmed in their supposition of the identity of the patriot, by an officer's publickly

asking him, in a seeming serious manner, how long he had been imprisoned, &c., and the Gentleman, in his answers, humourously personating Mr. Wilkes, the mob were not undeceived till he was gone.'
(Both of these passages have been reprinted in the Thoresby Society Publications, Vol. XXXVIII, Leeds, 1938.)

Another event which figures in accounts of the seventeenth century, the Popish Plot, may be taken as a further example of the use of local history in adding convincing detail to general accounts. This extract is from the Borough Records of Beverley, in the East Riding of Yorkshire (Yorkshire Archaeological Society, Record Series, Vol. LXXXIV).

18th November 1678. Ordered that, in respect of the present dangers by reason of a popish plot lately discovered, a watch be kept at the Beckside, Norwood, and the three barres every night until further order; the Mayor and Governors having had intelligence that several nights lately many horses have been heard passing the streets to and fro, but no account can be given of their business; and that two out of each ward be summoned night by night to keep the watch accordingly; a Governor and Burgess to take care to see that the watch be duly kept.

The intense fear of Catholics aroused at that time is more easily appreciated and understood when laid bare in such extracts from local records.

Local history is also valuable for the teacher of history in the use that can be made of tangible relics of the past. Most pupils of secondary school age, and certainly those of average and below average ability, are in Piagetian terms, still at the stage of concrete operational thinking. They can reason only in concrete situations where they are actively using material data which they can see and touch. It is not surprising, therefore, that such pupils find it difficult to understand the purely verbal accounts of most history books and lessons. Local history can very often supply the material data and concrete situations which such accounts lack. It can achieve this in several ways. Visits to some local historical site, a Roman villa or fort, a medieval church or castle, an eighteenth-century canal or a nineteenth-century factory, all these will bring pupils into contact with some tangible materials of the past upon which their thinking can operate. Visits to a museum will achieve a similar purpose, when carefully organized and when the pupils are provided with work-sheets (see below). Alternatively, relics of the past may be used in the classroom. Many local education authorities have a museum service through which relics, either original or reproduced, can be borrowed for classroom use. Often, too, models of buildings, tools or weapons used in the past, may be available on loan in this way. Individual teachers may also make their own models or acquire relics by field work in their own localities. Another way is to obtain photostat copies of documents from the local Record Office. These, with the help of a translation where necessary, can become a tangible object of history which pupils can use and understand. In these various ways local history can confront the pupils with that concrete material which they need at this stage in their development. Unless teachers of history realize this and prepare materials and lessons accordingly, then history in schools will remain what for many pupils it seems to be, a tale, not necessarily told by an idiot, but 'full of sound and fury, signifying nothing'.

In addition to its value in giving reality to remote historical generalizations and in providing pupils with tangible historical data, local history is also extremely valuable in the opportunities it offers for practical work, whether of groups or individuals. The following suggestions for practical work are not exhaustive, and they will need to be modified by the teacher's own experience and knowledge, the capabilities of the children and the availability of the records. No doubt teachers will be able to think of other activities but here are some possibilities for consideration.

1. *Parish registers*: trace common surnames and make a collection of local surnames of the present day for comparison; work out population changes and relate them to epidemics, poor harvests, enclosures, unemployment and public health measures like vaccination.

2. *Churchwardens' accounts*: trace repairs and restoration of the local church and combine with a visit to the church; trace the purchase of church furnishings, vestments and vessels and try to relate these to changes at the time of the Reformation; trace references to such national events as military victories, corona-tions and annual celebrations such as 5th November—all often marked by bell-ringing.

3. *Vestry minutes*: compare the duties of parish officers with those of modern Parish Councillors; trace entries relating to the control of plague, the destruction of vermin, the pollution of streams, and vaccination and compare these with modern public health measures.

4. *Accounts of Overseers of the Poor*: compile statistics of numbers of the poor and the methods of poor relief, noting the increasing expenditure over the years, and compare with modern relief by family allowances, pensions and national assistance.

5. *Records of Surveyors of the Highways*: use to trace changes in local roads, their provision and maintenance, and relate to wider themes, road building throughout Britain and the various changes in transport.

6. *Apprenticeship indentures*: useful in tracing local industries and in studying how poor and illegitimate children were treated.

7. *Settlement papers*: use to trace the mobility and occupations of the poor.

8. *Map work*: take a series of town or county maps (or photo-copies), from the sixteenth century to the present day and note the changes; from an enclosure map work out the position of the open fields before enclosure, this can then lead to field-work in which the children trace the visible remains of these fields such as old thick hedges, ridge and furrow, long fields and field names; using a tithe map, plot the land usage of the 1840s on a photocopy, and then con-struct a present-day land-usage map for comparison; using tithe and enclosure maps plot on a large-scale Ordnance Survey map of the locality the old field names and then find out present names and compare; make a map to show the age of the various buildings existing at the present in a town or rural area, using old maps, and building materials and styles to date them.

9. *Quarter Sessions Records*: use to make studies of the social life of past centuries, and particularly studies of crime and punishment; dramatize some of the cases and situations.

10. *School Records*: use log-books (often still at the school), managers' minutes and deeds to discover the history and life of early elementary schools; make a map and list showing the growth in school provision.

11. *Domesday Survey*: from the information given in the survey draw a map of the local area as it might have been in 1086, plotting for example, the mill, the church, the meadow land and the houses of the various villagers; work out the population figures of the

40

locality from the survey (multiply the number of households by five); construct a map to show the holdings of the different land-lords in a limited local area; dramatize a Domesday Inquest; study a modern farm or area and record the information in Domesday-fashion.

12. *Newspapers*: compile extracts from past newspapers of the locality and use them to reconstruct the social life of some past period, or to produce a 'line of development' study of some particular topic (such as transport, medicine or education), or to illustrate national history.

13. *Commercial Directories*: use to compile statistics and graphs to show the growth and/or decline of the various trades, professions, shops and industries of the locality.

14. *Buildings*: visits to the local parish church, abbey, castle, or Tudor and Georgian residences can be used to begin studies of the development of architecture, ecclesiastical, military and civil. Such visits provide numerous opportunities for practical work such as the drawing of the plans of buildings, sketches of notable features, monuments or ornaments, maps and charts to show the origin and use of the various building materials, and diagrams to show the reasons for the siting of particular buildings in specific places, and also perhaps to show the landscape alterations which have gone on. Furthermore, all these practical activities can become the starting points for discussion about the social scene and the people who lived, fought and worshipped in these buildings. In this connection the 'Get to Know' Series published by Methuen & Co. Ltd. is particularly helpful in providing guides for the exploration of both buildings and the landscape.

15. *Church Memorials*: these may be used to study social life in general, and are particularly useful for the study of costume and armour. Gravestones outside a church and tombs and mural tablets inside can be sketched and their details noted so that a study of the changes in styles of memorial tablets and tombs can be built up. Sometimes, memorials have been made by cutting human figures and inscriptions into brass, and these *brasses* have then been let into the surface of a stone slab or affixed to a wall. They were very common between the thirteenth and seventeenth centuries and they are very valuable in providing information about the costumes and armour of those centuries. Pupils can easily be taught to make and collect 'rubbings' of brasses. In the same way

D

41

that the head on a penny can be rubbed through paper with a pencil, so with sheets of white lining paper and thick black crayon or cobbler's heelball, 'rubbings' may be made of the monumental brasses.

16. *Visits to museums and historical sites*: visits should be part of a term's work—not just a jaunt—and prior to the visit lessons should be given on the historical background relevant to the museum or the site. It is also advisable for the teacher to make a prior visit to find out, if it is a site, its history, its plan and the remains to be seen, and, if it is a museum, the range of its rooms and their exhibits. The best way to use such a visit is to make it one in which a class 'finds out for itself' with the help of worksheets—and these need careful preparation beforehand.

WORKSHEETS FOR MUSEUMS

These may include a plan of the interior of the museum, which indicates the various rooms where pupils should go, lists of objects to look for and instructions as to what to find out about them, whether to draw them or write notes on them or both, whether to find out how specific objects 'worked' and whether to label their respective parts.

Examples:

i. Draw the following New Stone Age tools: an axe-head, a knife and a scraper all with wooden handles. (The handles will have decayed and so you must imagine them.)

ii. Find evidence that people who lived in the Iron Age spun, wove, grew corn and had horses and carts. N.B. The class would need to have learnt something of these processes beforehand.

iii. For study of museum exhibits of the Roman period, a class might be divided into groups each studying different topics such as home life, weapons, farming, trades, pottery and coins.

iv. A similar approach could be used with later periods of history, and topics such as costume, hair styles and furniture might be added.

WORKSHEETS FOR SITES

These may include a plan of the site, lists of objects and places pupils could put on the plan, and drawings of mosaics, or styles of architecture or decorative motifs for the pupils to look out for and locate.

Examples:

i. On the castle plan provided mark the position of the draw-bridge, the keep and the kitchens.

ii. On the plan of a Roman villa or camp mark in the position of the baths, the granaries and the kitchens.

iii. On the plan of a church mark the position of the piscina, the rood and the font, or show by using different colours which parts of the church belong to the Norman, Decorated and Perpendicular periods.

iv. Using the cyclostyled drawings of decorative motifs as a guide find examples in this church of ball-flower ornament, dog-tooth ornament, corbels and a string course.

v. Similar worksheets might be devised to study types of wood-work in a building, or silverware on show in a country mansion, or the features of an Adam room in a country house.

vi. Make an 'age-of-buildings' map of a village that the class may visit.

It is also important to follow up the visit by work in school. For example, if it is ensured that the relevant books and pictures are available, the children can (*a*) make individual, group or class books on some subject, (*b*) make charts, friezes and models or dress dolls, (*c*) prepare individual talks to give to the rest of the class. The teacher too can follow up the visit in lessons which bring out its wider significance. For example a visit to a Roman villa in Britain could be put in the context of Roman life in Italy and in the Roman Empire as a whole.

17. Compile a history of recent times from local sources: use written material such as local newspapers but also employ the children to make recordings, either written or on tape, of the witness and memories of parents, grandparents and older people of the neighbourhood.

George Ewart Evans's book *Ask the Fellows who Cut the Hay* (Faber) is an excellent example of what might be done in this way.

Before children can engage in any of these suggested activities with effect, preparation by the teacher is essential. It takes time and effort but these are amply repaid in the interest it brings for both pupils and teacher. The very act of handling old documents serves to close the gap of centuries and the people of the past take on a life and reality which is so often absent in textbook accounts. Such activities also give children the challenge and responsibility of independent work as well as the experience of co-operating with others in some team research.

It would be foolish, however, to imagine that local history is the answer to the history teacher's prayer. It presents problems of class management, for finding out 'on the ground' or in a records office is not an easy or natural process for school children, nor is it the learning environment to which they are accustomed. Another difficulty arises from the fact that there are few schools whose immediate locality provides enough historical material to illustrate a wide range of general history. A small town may have its castle and abbey near and so provide an excellent stimulus for the study of medieval history, but be quite lacking in material which might make more realistic the pre-1832 franchise. Moreover, in connection with this it should be remembered that events which occurred in the locality of a pupil's school are not necessarily any nearer to his or her experience than events which happened two hundred miles away. Local history is not some instant mix which immediately delights the tastes of children so that they cry for more. But, on the whole, in using local history teachers do proceed on the sound educational principle of moving from the known to the unknown.

5. Methods and Materials–I

So far this book has been concerned mainly with syllabus-making, with discussion about what sorts of history we should teach, whether medieval or recent history, local, national or world history. In such a debate it is possible for history teachers to take up different positions, but when it comes to the practice of teaching, all are faced with very similar problems; the problems of presenting a subject which is about the dead to children who are concerned only with the immediate problems of living.

The subject of history presents those who would teach it with a major problem, peculiar to itself and less familiar to teachers of many other subjects. It is essentially a problem of *resurrection*, of how to make the dead live, the intangible tangible, the past present. A know-ledgeable teacher with imaginative narrative powers or with visual aids of various kinds can do a great deal to achieve this difficult task.

There is, however, another factor in the total problem of teaching history. If the subject itself presents difficulties the nature and abilities of the pupils presents others which are just as hard to overcome. Before any suggestions are made about methods and materials a prior task is to consider further the characteristics of pupils of average and below-average ability as they appear to the teacher in the classroom. Their powers of concentration are limited and they cannot absorb very much of anything, be it information, ideas or experiences, at any one time; they can deal better with particular issues and specific examples rather than with abstract ideas and generalities.

The thought of the great majority of children up to the age of about 16 does not advance beyond the concrete operational stage, this is a vital factor governing the choice of language—as well as guiding the selection of topics—for the history lesson. It is essential to avoid abstractions and to be as concrete as possible; this can be particularly difficult to manage in teaching history because the nature of the material so often makes it convenient for the mature historian to think—and therefore to express himself—in abstract terms. A brief survey of the language used in many of the text books found in secondary schools makes this only too clear. The following passage is from a well-known book intended for boys and girls of about 15.

Holy Russia. The peasants for whom everything was to be done were themselves the most conservative force in Europe—not cynically conservative like Metternich; or sentimentally conservative, like the Prussian Junkers; but unreflectingly so because they were almost incapable of imagining a different and a better world. Unable to read or write, they had no ideas beyond the life of their own villages, sparsely scattered among the dark forests and rich plains of Russia. Two loyalties alone made a man of the peasant. The first was his devotion to the church; a fierce, passionate devotion undisturbed by the slightest suspicion of doubt. No whispers of the struggles between Catholic and Protestant, between believers and atheists, had ever reached his knowledge. To the Russian peasant the teaching of the Orthodox church was as unquestioned as the routine of agriculture. His second loyalty was to the Tsar, the 'autocrat of all the Russias', the anointed of God who was the 'little father' of all his people. Church and throne stood together in the peasants' mind.

Many of the political and economic concepts which lie behind the more concrete material which is being taught are bound to arise in the course of discussion during history lessons and many of these are themselves abstract; equality, democracy, conservatism, *laissez-faire* and protection—when words such as these arise there is no alternative but to attempt to explain in terms as meaningful as possible and with examples as concrete as possible.

It must also be remembered that the meaning of even fairly commonplace words involving little abstraction to pupils with their limited experience may be very different from their meaning to the teacher. This is a problem for teachers generally; the experience of life of boys and girls in schools is so much more restricted than that of adults that it is essential for teachers to ask themselves just what their pupils' experience is likely to have been, in what way they will have become familiar with certain words and what those words will therefore mean to them. There are really two limitations which the history teacher has to bear in mind, first the limited meaning conveyed by particular words, and secondly, the comparatively small vocabulary of pupils. This latter limitation is often especially marked in the case of children from less cultured homes and who for various reasons often seem to be more than adequately represented among the less able.

The home background often leads to quite different meanings being attached to words. It is fairly clear that there will be differences between boys and girls of rural and urban backgrounds. A common word such as *countryside* may well conjure up pleasant memories of holidays and trips to the country to an urban child; a cowman's son is more likely to think of it as a place from which one desires to escape to the amenities of the city. A teacher moving from an upland area in the north of England to another rural area in East Anglia would find that the word 'farm' conjured up very different concepts in the minds of his pupils. It is a good deal easier to teach boys and girls about the enclosures of the eighteenth century in areas that experienced such enclosures than it is in other districts where the local topography would clearly have made the traditional open-field system impossible at any time.

Teachers also need to ensure that the meanings of words which describe apparently solid physical things that pupils will be familiar with have not changed considerably. Terms such as mine, textile mill or factory may well bring to the contemporary mind something on a scale so much more vast as to be quite unlike anything the teacher will wish to suggest if he is describing industrial developments in the late eighteenth century.

The contemporary environment in which they have to live has had other effects also on the understanding of pupils and on the ways in which they learn. Television and mass advertising techniques have encouraged a greater visual awareness, while the radio has also helped to condition the young to audio machines. These are characteristics which teachers need to bear in mind in devising their methods of approach.

The suggestions concerning methods and materials which follow take into account these factors. They are based on the need which the less able have for concrete material, their reliance on their audio-visual senses and their capacity to respond to a good story. But whatever techniques may be suggested or adopted, it must not be forgotten that the core of the problem is to persuade pupils to make an active effort to learn. There is a sense in which teaching is a secondary function aimed at encouraging the primary function of learning by the individual pupil; any lack of ability in pupils makes this not less but more important. It is not a case of making charitable provision for the less able, but of trying to help them to become more able. The point is put succinctly in the old Chinese proverb: 'Give a man a fish and you have fed him for a day; teach him how to fish and you have fed him for a long time.'

Teaching what History is

That the first stage in the teaching of any subject should be to show the pupils what that subject is so that they may relate it to their personal needs seems fairly obvious and yet rarely do history teachers begin in this way. Rather the stuff of history is produced and the pupils wade into it as into a haystack. It is assumed that on their way the pupils will pick up conceptions of what history is, of how historians work and of the value of history as a study. To take an opposite course and begin with carefully structured lessons on the nature of history as a mode of inquiry seems to be shunned by historians as anathema, and this is true, not only of history teachers at the secondary school level but sometimes also in colleges of education and universities. The reason for this prevailing attitude would seem to be the view that doing something is better than talking about how to do it and such a view may have some validity. Nevertheless, even if the game's the thing it must be recognized that few will play a game without first wanting to know the point of it, that there are goals to be scored, 'tricks' to be won, or 'a King' to be checkmated. Similarly with history. If pupils—and this applies particularly for those who are less able—are to follow their courses of history with interest, they must see what it is all about, they must see the point of it.

The suggestion here is that the first and main method of teaching history is to teach it as it is known to historians as a way of finding out, of selecting and of writing about events in the past. For historians, history is not the recitation of memorized facts, the reliance on one text-book account, or the supplying of relevant missing words to some emasculated account. Yet this is what it can become in school. The consequence is that many pupils dislike history without, paradoxically enough, ever having known it. The remedy then is to teach history as it is and two general suggestions may be made about this. First there should be introductory lessons about what history is, reinforced in any course which follows by frequent discussions about the tasks and techniques of the historian. Pupils in school should

48

PLATE V

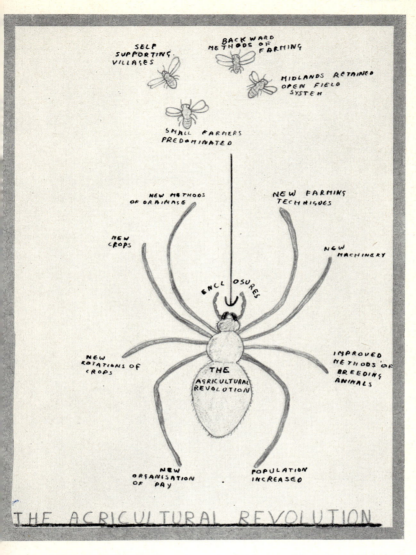

PLATE V: Spider and flies diagram drawn by a 13 year-old pupil to illustrate the Agricultural Revolution (*see page* 53)

PLATES VI–VIII (over page): Individual task cards used with pupils of 11, 12 and 13 years of age (*see page* 53)

PLATE VI

This man was one of the murderers of Archbishop
Thomas Becket.

1. Find out the story of the murder.

2. Design and write a 'Police Wanted' notice for
   this man.

3. Write a newspaper report,with headlines,
   of either a) the murder

        or   b) the penance which Henry II did.

PLATE VII

Look carefully at this 14th century harvest scene.

1. Describe the three harvesting jobs which are illustrated here.

   How do they differ from harvesting today?

2. What could the pack-horse be used for in the Middle Ages?

3. Imagine you are a medieval farmer and make a list of all the buildings, livestock and tools you would have on your farm.

PLATE VIII

1. Make a copy of this picture of a medieval watermill
2. Find the various parts and label them on your picture
   a) the water wheel
   b) the wooden gearing which transmits the driving power to the millstones. You can see it through the wheel.
   c) the millstones
   d) the hopper above the millstones for feeding in the corn
3. Where would the mill be sited in a medieval village?
4. Why was the miller so important in a medieval village?

pursue activities which are genuinely akin to those of the professional historian. For example, they should pursue finding-out tasks, tasks that involve interpretation, tasks that demand attempts at reliving men's thoughts and feelings in past situations, and finally tasks of narrative and reconstruction of the past in words, written or spoken, in pictures or in models.

A Scheme for Introducing the Study of History

1. *Man's need of history*:

(*a*) History satisfies the basic human need for an identity. Everyone has an image or picture of the sort of person he is—or thinks he is. When we meet someone else for the first time, we consciously or subconsciously try to make some sort of impression; as we get to know them better we tend to talk about ourselves and our background, where we have lived, what occupations we have followed, etc. In speaking of these things we build up in the other person's mind a history of ourselves. This personal history is fundamental to the individual's personality.

In the same way that individuals have their personal histories, so groups of people such as clubs, societies, companies, unions and local districts tend to have corporate images of themselves based upon their members' concepts of their achievement and position, i.e. on their histories. This corporate image based upon a concept of an organization's history is something so strong that the company or union will arrange to publish a history of itself. The nation with its national history is a rather special example of a group with a group image.

(*b*) One possible approach to this is through the family of the pupil, father's and mother's occupations; grandparents' occupations, where the various parts of the family come from.

2. *Records or sources of history*:

(*a*) Types

    i. Objects men have made or used, from pots and pans to jewellery and paintings;

    ii. writings which men have produced in the course of their work or in their private lives, such as letters, plans, memoranda, reports, wills, accounts, advertisements, newspapers, pamphlets and books;

iii. accounts written by eye-witnesses or by those who got their information from eye-witnesses, contemporary histories.

(*b*) A typical exercise might be: 'If we want to find out how men lived in Ancient Egypt what kinds of records might there be to help us? Make a list. Now make another list of the records we could use to find out how people lived there in 1900. What are the main differences between the two lists?'

3. *Evidence*: the different kinds of evidence and the historian's problem of interpreting it.

(*a*) Discussion of an imaginary present-day situation will provide material for the classification of the different kinds of evidence. For example: 'Imagine we are looking at the evidence which a policeman has taken at the scene of a road accident. He has taken evidence from the following people; the driver, the driver's wife who was with him in the car, the injured 5-year-old boy, the boy's mother who was not present when the accident occurred, the boy's companion, aged 8 years, who was present, a man who was 150 yards farther up the road who saw the accident but who suffered from short-sightedness and was not wearing his spectacles at the time, two women who were gossiping near to where the accident occurred. Make a list of these people in the order in which you think their evidence would be the most reliable and give reasons for your choice.'

Or another example which offers greater differentiation of the kinds of evidence. 'Consider the following statement: "On Saturday Scotland beat England at football by one goal to nil. The goal came from a well-deserved penalty given when the England full-back fouled the Scottish centre-forward." Make a list of the various sources of knowledge we might go to in order to verify this report (for example, a newspaper report, an English spectator at the game but a small man and well back in the crowd, a person who saw the match on television, the English goalkeeper, a Scottish supporter who was at the match, the account recorded on tape of the radio commentator made at the time of the incident) and say how you would assess their reliability.'

(*b*) The difference between what historians call primary and secondary source materials can be discussed at a simple level.

(*c*) The ways in which historians verify the authenticity of objects from the past can be considered. For example, before deciding that a vase came from Roman times, historians would want to check where it was found and make sure that the materials from which it was made, the style in which it was made and its present condition were similar to those of vases which were already known to be Roman.

4. *Explanation in history*: the historian tries to explain the changes that have occurred in man's life in the past and the events that have happened by discussing 'causes' and 'consequences'. Some understanding of what these words can mean may be gained by discussion of such situations as the following:

'He stole the bread because he was hungry.'

'He wanted an exciting life so he joined the army.'

'He became a doctor because he wanted to help people and because it was a better paid job than teaching.'

'The boy had hit his sister so he pushed him into the stream and then the fight began.'

'Her friend in Paris had sent her pictures of these new clothes and so she decided to make some for herself just like them.'

Many of these apparently simple statements come close to sophisticated historical explanations of the causes of crusades, explorations and wars, or of the consequences of actions and contacts.

5. *Time*: events happen in time and in history they are labelled with dates to mark the order in which they happened.

(*a*) Systems of dating

The Romans reckoned from the year of the founding of their city.

We date all events from the birth of Jesus Christ, events before being styled B.C. and those after A.D.

(*b*) Conventional divisions of the history of Europe and the Near East—approximate and artificial.

Ancient Times—from the beginning to the break-up of the Roman Empire. A.D. 450.

Medieval Times—its earlier part often called the Dark Ages because of its neglect of ancient learning, the whole running from A.D. 450 to about A.D. 1500.

Renaissance and Reformation Times—to about 1700.

Modern Times—beginning with the acceptance of the scientific outlook.

51

6. Methods and Materials–II

Some Activities for Pupils

Since teaching is really causing others to learn, the teacher's problem is one of devising learning tasks so that each pupil can learn for himself or herself. This problem of how to individualize learning becomes an increasingly pressing one as, in more and more schools, teachers are confronted by classes of mixed abilities. The suggestions for pupil activities which follow have three characteristics. First they are akin to those activities which mature and professional historians engage in. They differ not in kind but in degree from mature historical skills. In this way they are in tune with J. S. Bruner's now famous hypothesis 'that any subject can be taught effectively in some intellectually honest form to any child at any stage of development' (*The Process of Education*, Harvard University Press, 1962) and his central conviction 'that intellectual activity anywhere is the same, whether at the frontier of knowledge or in a third-grade classroom'. Secondly, they are activities which individualize learning. Some, it is true, may lead to or may demand co-operation within a group but all involve individual learning tasks. Thirdly, they present the pupils with concrete material and with visual stimulus and some give opportunities for work with tape recorders. In other words, they attempt to meet the needs and characteristics of the pupils themselves.

1. *Individual Task Cards*

To fulfil the need of the less able pupils for limited and specific tasks rather than general ones such as 'find out about transport', and to help overcome that difficult problem for the class-teacher, namely the differing pace at which the children work, individual task cards are invaluable. It is advisable to make sets of these cards offering tasks of varying difficulty for the various periods of history on the school syllabus. They take time to make, but once made they last a considerable length of time and they have great advantages for the pupils. First, they enable each pupil to be given a task suited to his ability. Secondly the pupil can work at his own pace. Thirdly the pupil gains the sense of achievement in completing a task and also the incentive to go on to another. Finally if a pupil completes a series of well-planned cards he cannot help but discover and understand a wide range of topics within any particular period. The cards can be made with pictures or information taken from a variety of sources such as B.B.C. pamphlets, newspapers, *Pictorial Education* and picture postcards. Examples of these task cards are illustrated on Plates VI, VII and VIII.

2. *Diagrams*

Pupils can be helped in their learning if they are encouraged to find out and digest material on specific topics by attempting to portray it diagrammatically. For this method involves pupils in classifying and ordering their material and in presenting it as a historical explanation. The example shown in Plate V is the work of one boy who was asked to present what he had learned of changes in agriculture in England during the eighteenth century. This example is more imaginative than most from the class, but the exercise had its value even for those who produced line diagrams or copied the 'tree-diagram' which the teacher had employed to illustrate a topic earlier in the school year.

3. *Time Charts*

One concept which presents children with considerable difficulties is that of time. Their experience of time is obviously very limited and a school term can seem like an eternity. The use of the most simple form of time chart can help to overcome this difficulty. A line of time is a straightforward way of representing visually a period of time and it is a very useful way of enabling pupils to get some idea of the relative length of different periods. If a child merely hears that event A happened 1000 years ago and event B 10,000 years ago, the greater lapse of time between the two events than between event A and the present day tends to go unobserved; all such a verbal statement usually succeeds in conveying is that both events happened a very long time ago. A line of time will help to put these periods of time in perspective.

The time chart is a useful device for illustrating the correct sequence of events and for bringing out the possible relationship between events. The very terseness of a chart makes it a useful medium for sorting out a complicated jumble of incidents. The charts themselves can take a variety of forms, but they do lose something of their value if they become too complex.

53

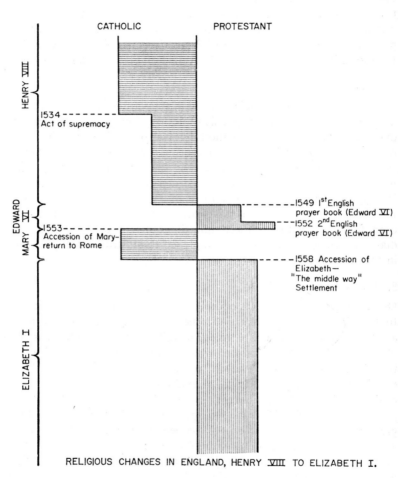

RELIGIOUS CHANGES IN ENGLAND, HENRY VIII TO ELIZABETH I.

Example of Time Chart (*page* 53).

4. *Strip-Cartoons*

Cartoons in strip form, perhaps using pin-head figures, are a useful way in which pupils, particularly the less able, can present what they have learned. For example, instead of the exercise 'Write an account of life in a medieval monastery' may be substituted this, 'Draw pictures of medieval monks, in the infirmary, gardening, looking after sheep, at worship'.

5. *Duplicated Pictures*

Duplicated outline pictures of notable historical characters, situations or events, are also useful. Pupils can cut them out, colour them, paste them in their own books and make them a visual centre of their record of what they have learned. Some pupils will be able to write an account of some length on the subject of the pictures; others may be able to offer no more than a caption.

6. *Map Work*

Maps may be used in a variety of ways by all secondary school pupils whether able or less able. They are a visual and concrete way of recording what has been learned. Four ways in which they may be used are:

(*a*) To record military campaigns.
(*b*) To plot routes. e.g. 'Which countries would Nelson sail past on his way to Egypt?'
(*c*) 'On an outline map of the Roman Empire mark in from a modern map the countries which were once included within the territory of that Empire.'
(*d*) To plot towns or areas which had a political or economic significance, e.g. the cloth producing towns of medieval England or the areas which, in general, supported Parliament in the English Civil War.

7. *Modelling*

This is valuable in that it is a concrete activity which produces visual and tangible records of the past for pupils to consider. Much of it is best done out of school lesson-time. For example the making of 'Airfix' or similar models and the dressing of dolls in historical costume is probably best done out of class—at home or in the dinner hour—and the finished models displayed in school. Models in wood, cardboard or plasticine, of houses, castles or settlements of the past could, however, be made, either wholly or partly, in lesson-time. Modelling is especially valuable in the study of certain periods of history. For example, a lesson spent moulding clay pots much as Neolithic men or women would have made them is a task of historical re-creation which will give pupils a far better understanding of what life was like in the Stone Age than any verbal account or discussion could give. Another valuable 'modelling' lesson is one which gives pupils a taste of the restoration work an archaeologist might perform on some fragmented pot he has found. Few can find pieces of a red Samian ware Roman vase and stick them together to restore it, but all teachers can get a bowlful of old crockery, break it into pieces and then let a group of pupils find and fit the pieces together. In this way they may only restore a 1965 jug or a 1945 saucer but the experience is similar to the recovery of an antique Roman vase.

8. *Written Work*

Most of our pupils of average and below average ability cannot write at length. They lack a fluent command of written English. Nevertheless the history teacher should give them an opportunity to practise such powers of writing that they have, particularly in the writing of imaginative accounts. The teacher can also help them by giving them props and pointers in the form of vocabulary and ideas to enable them to produce a written account of some topic they have studied (Plates III and IV).

(*a*) One method, which is often used in schools, is the missing-word exercise. The pupils are given sentences or short passages describing events or characters of historical importance in which certain key words are omitted. The pupil has to copy out the passage supplying the missing words either from memory, by searching them out from a textbook, or by choosing the relevant one from a list provided by the teacher. For example:

'Soon after . . . had died Harold became king. First he had to march . . . to meet Harald . . . He defeated the Norseman in battle at . . . . Meanwhile Duke . . . had landed his army on the . . . coast near . . . . The English army marched south and on September 28th . . . the two armies met in battle. After a long struggle the . . . eventually won mainly because of the superior strength of their . . . . In the battle . . . was killed and . . . now became king.'

(cavalry, Hastings, William, north, Edward, Hardrada, Normans, Harold, Sussex, Stamford Bridge, 1066.)

Though such an exercise does offer help to the less able pupils and enables them to complete at least one paragraph of continuous prose it is probably too often employed in schools. It has value as an occasional exercise or as a type of objective test but if it becomes the regular diet for the less able its effect is cramping and stultifying.

(*b*) Many less able pupils will be quite incapable of writing 'An account of the effects of the Norman Conquest' in essay form. Imaginative accounts written in the first persons are in any case far more valuable at this stage. Even these, however, will often be beyond the capabilities of some pupils. Certainly pupils who have seemed incapable of formal, sustained written work have produced pieces of imaginative writing which revealed a deeply sympathetic understanding of the past. Letters, diaries, newspaper reports, all written 'on the spot' bring children into a personal relationship with the past and the interest, understanding and quality of achievement which often results make these very valuable exercises. The following examples are the work of fourth-form girls of very modest ability in a secondary modern school. The class had seen a film on the first World War and were then asked to write letters home describing conditions in the trenches.

i. Dear Family,

This is the first chance I had to write you a letter. The conditions here are terrific there are mangled bodies everywhere the guns never seem to stop booming. The rain comes flowing into the trenches mixed with the blood from shattered bodies piled 10 ft. high rotting in no man's land. Everyday is full of sadness, not a day goes by without us finding the body of one of our friends. Last week George Webb and I were having a laugh at a private joke and George moved a little to look over the top of the trench, when all at once I heard a shot and George slumped towards me, when I saw what used to be his face I nearly died, his eyes were no longer there he had no nose or mouth all that I saw was a mass of blood bone and bits of teeth. My hands were full of shattered skin and my clothes were soaking with his blood. I layed on my stomach and crept as far away as I could and I broke down and wept. I will

E

never forget that as long as I live. I will try to write more often, I wish with all my heart that this terrible war would end.

All my love to the family
from your loving son Matthew

ii. Dear Mother and father and sister

I have now been posted to the trench unit I dont like it at all. It is so cold and dirty. It as just begun to snow, and it is very very cold my hands are so cold I can hardley move I wish I were again the fire at home. The uniform we have been given is so cold my overcoat got torn on the barbed wire and we haven't been back to the barracks we are fighting all the time every minet every second hour. The conditions are shocking. The rain came the other day so hard we are walking around the trenches in 2–3 inches of mud. I will close now because I ear the enemy Tanks approaching

Good bye for now
Mother xx Your dear son Paul

P.S. I will try to keep away from the enemy.

(c) If note-making and written accounts of historical events are expected from the less able pupils then they must be guided. There are two main ways of approaching this. Either headings (names, dates, etc.) can be given to the pupils as a basis for their work, or questions can be asked of them in such a way that the answers which the pupils produce will provide a series of notes or a written account of some topic. In the fourth year and fifth year there may be place for the guided essay. It is not enough to ask pupils of average and less-than-average ability to write an essay or to prepare a set of notes, they need much help especially in their first attempts. This help can be given in the form of paragraph headings and in suggestions of content for each paragraph. For example:

Essay—The Effects of Stalin's Rule in Russia, 1924–1939.

Use the headings and your answers to the questions to form paragraphs.

Paragraph 1. Death of Lenin—when?—left two challengers for leadership of Russia. Who were they? What had they done so far for Russia and what was their position? Suggest at least two reasons why they quarrelled. How did they differ in policy? How did their struggle for power end? Who won?

Paragraph 2. Stalin's 'Five-Year Plans'. The idea behind them—state control and five-year production targets for industries. Which industries were made to develop the most? What were the incentives to make the workers work hard? Give some production figures to show the success of the plans.

Paragraph 3. What was the plan for agriculture? Was there opposition to the plan? How was the plan carried through? Was it successful?

Paragraph 4. How was Russia ruled at this time? How was the Council of Ministers elected? Was there much freedom for the ordinary citizen? What did the NKVD do? How was education affected? What happened to the Church?

Paragraph 5. The 'purge' 1934–37 brought Stalin complete power. Do you agree he had achieved much for Russia?

9. *Dramatic Work*

This has a double value for less able pupils. Firstly it is another way of involving them at a personal and imaginative level with history and secondly it provides them with an opportunity to express themselves orally which often comes more easily to such pupils than written expression. Dramatic work may take a variety of forms.

(*a*) The dramatization of historical situations such as a medieval manorial court or a meeting of historical characters such as Henry VIII and Archbishop Cranmer discussing the divorce of Catherine of Aragon, or Hitler and Mussolini discussing their desires for territorial expansion. The dramatizations can be spontaneous or from scripts which the pupils have prepared either by themselves or with the teacher's help.

(*b*) Dramatizations which a group have prepared and recorded on tape can be effectively communicated to the rest of the class. Or occasionally as a project the whole class might co-operate in a 'mock' radio programme on some historical sequence such as the murder of Thomas Becket, the Spanish Armada, the Great Fire of London or Peterloo. This would involve narratives of the background, on-the-spot interviews of the main characters (best done spontaneously) and discussion by commentators, all recorded on tape with visual aids made to accompany the recording.

(c) Some of our less able pupils will be fluent enough readers to cope with dramatized scripts written by the teacher or with published historical dramatizations such as those appearing in *Dramatic Decisions, 1776–1945* by John H. Bowles (Macmillan, 1961) or the four volumes of *History in Action* by Alan Hill and Susan Ault (Heinemann, 1964). Though such readings are not the children's own creative work, they are not to be despised since they involve pupils in historical situations and extend their imaginations.

The use of dramatic work in history teaching has its hazards. It is not recommended for example to teachers who are still struggling to control their classes. On the other hand the very interest and attention which dramatic work itself engenders will often—though not always—serve to diminish problems of class control. The cautionary tale which follows tells its own story (from *History as a School of Citizenship*, H. M. Madeley, 1920):

> Tom Brown, a boy who seldom tries
> Was taught by me to dramatize
> He acted Brutus to the life
> And killed Joe Turner with a knife,
> Of course, he overdid the part
> But's that's not what I took to heart
> I think it was a beastly shame
> To say 'The Teacher was to blame'.

10. *Using Books*

The tradition of issuing a copy of the same book to each pupil in a class seems to be passing in some schools. The disadvantages of the traditional system are that reliance on one textbook tends to circumscribe the year's work and that the issuing of the one book encourages an uncritical acceptance of the written word—a very unfortunate consequence. It is far better if various sets of books, such as textbooks and simple biographies, can be made available in the history room for pupils to use as they need them. Fortunately an increasing number of books suitable for children to use in this way are becoming available from publishers.

The Importance of Story

Guiding pupils in their learning activities is one side of the teacher's work; another side is the direct exposition of the subject in ways that engage the interest and attention of the pupils. In history teaching this latter task is more likely to be achieved if history is presented as a story. In all the discussion about whether history is an art or a science and about the nature of historical explanation the central point that emerges in that story is the essence of history. This is fortunate for the history teacher in that his subject can take a form which should have ready appeal to pupils of all ages and abilities.

Some teachers are born story-tellers. They have a good memory for detail, a fluent and sensitive use of vocabulary which enables them to produce the right word at the right time, a voice too well modulated ever to become monotonous, and sometimes—though hardly an essential quality—a certain capacity for histrionics. A teacher who lacks such characteristics by grace need not despair for they may be acquired, at least to a certain degree, by practice and application. Certainly for a history teacher the ability to tell a good story is worth acquiring for the telling or reading of stories of the past remains a central method in the teaching of history. It was true when a Renaissance schoolmaster like Vittorino da Feltre told stories of the history of the Romans, or when Thomas Arnold taught history, and it remains true today. What has changed is the variety and provision of aids which the history teacher can now employ to illustrate his story of the past. For example, it is now comparatively easy to find in print collections of documentary source material some of which can be duplicated on school premises and then given to the pupils as an illustration of some point in the story which the teacher is unfolding. In telling the story of factory life and reform in England in the nineteenth century the following extract, for example, is particularly useful.

Evidence given before Select Committee on Children in Factories, 1832

What age did you go into the mill?—about 9 years old.
What sort of position do you stand in, in order to piece worsted goods?—If we are higher than the frames we have to bend our bodies and our legs so: (here the witness showed the position in which he worked). Have you always to bend your body?—Yes always.
Were you a healthy and strong boy before you went to the mill?—Yes.
Could you walk well?—Yes; I could walk from Leeds to Bradford when I was 8 years old.
Without any pain or difficulty?—Yes.

You felt no fatigue from it?—Not much.

How long did you work at that mill for those long hours before you found your limbs began to fail?—About a year.

Did it come on with great pain?—It did.

Have you ever been beaten?—Yes, till I was black and blue on my face; and had my ears torn.

Were you generally beaten at the end of the day more than at any other time?—Yes; at the latter end, when we grew tired and fatigued.

Will you have the goodness to show the Committee your limbs? (the witness did so and they appeared to be excessively crooked).

Can you stand at all without crutches?—Not without crutches or a stick, or something to lean against.

Can you walk at all?—No.

Can you get up stairs?—Perhaps I might creep up.

Must it be upon your hands and knees?—Yes, or backwards way.

Do you get up stairs backwards way?—Yes, every night.

(Evidence of Benjamin, aged 16, who worked at Mr. Cozen's Mill, Bowling Lane, Bradford.)

A valuable source of documentary material is the series entitled *They Saw it Happen* published by Basil Blackwell.

The visual illustration of history is not only easy to effect but it may be crucial if learning is to take place. There is some evidence to suggest that while we remember only some 15 per cent of what we hear, we remember some 75 per cent of what we see and hear. Certainly the young nowadays are used to responding to visual means of communication in an age when cinemas and television in most homes make films a familiar sight. In presenting history the teacher has many visual means at his disposal. Maps and pictures to illustrate most of the general topics in the history of the past can now be bought commercially. Alternatively maps or diagrams to illustrate specific topics can be drawn by teachers themselves and these are often more effective than commercial productions which sometimes try to portray too much at once. The *History Class Pictures* published by Macmillan & Co. are comprehensive in their range. *Pictorial Education* is another useful source of historical illustrations. It seems to be more often used in primary schools than in secondary schools though its coverage is not too elementary for secondary school use and its value for the less able pupils alone would certainly justify its regular purchase. The *Jackdaw* folders published by Jonathan Cape are also useful in this connection. Teachers will find that they vary in suitability for use with pupils of average and below-average ability. Some of them provide excellent illustrations for class use, while others incorporate material which can be used only with small groups of fairly able children. Another generous source of historical pictures is the *Britain's Story told in Pictures* series by C. W. Airne and published by Hope & Hudson. In addition to these paper illustrations, films, film strips and photographic slides can aid the history teacher. With film strips and slides care has to be taken that they are used to illustrate a story which the teacher is presenting and do not themselves determine the course of the lesson. This is perhaps best done by showing only a few slides or frames of a film strip at any one time and by ensuring that the pupils actively appreciate their illustrative worth by questioning them and commenting on the illustrations. A third kind of historical illustrative material is the object or model. An oral lesson on life at a Roman villa would be very fully illustrated if the teacher not only introduced an outline plan and a photograph of a hypocaust, but also produced in class for all to see and touch part of a Roman flue tile. Such objects and models illustrating all the various periods of history may be found, bought, begged or borrowed from the local Schools Museum Services which exist in many parts of the country. Another visual means of illustrating historical stories, particularly accounts of military or naval campaigns, is a magnetic board. These can be easily made from a sheet of galvanized metal, with one side painted blue as a background to illustrations of naval movements and the other green for military manoeuvres. The moving pieces can be made from polystyrene and the small magnets fixed to the back of the pieces with some self-adhesive tape. The pieces may be painted to distinguish opposing sides. There is an illustration of a home-made magnetic board on Plates IX and X.

The gramophone record player and the tape recorder can also help the teacher of history in providing audio-illustrations of historical accounts. The *Modern Times* series of books published by Longmans have accompanying records which provide sound illustrations of the characters and events discussed in the books. Some recording companies have produced specifically historical records such as the one on Oliver Cromwell produced by H.M.V. while the series of ballads and sea-songs produced by Topic Recording Company can be used to illustrate various themes in the history of Britain. Apart from this direct use of gramophone records the tape recorder can be very useful in a history lesson. It can be used to select and edit sound illustrations taken from records or from the radio and it can be used to record readings of documentary sources, dramatizations and sound effects produced by the teacher and his pupils themselves and replayed at the relevant moment in any history lesson. For example the extract of evidence given before the Select Committee on Children in Factories, 1832, which is reproduced on page 61, would gain as an illustration if it were pre-recorded and played on tape as a dialogue.

Little need be said about the excellent services offered to teachers and pupils by the sound and television programmes of the B.B.C. and the Independent Television Companies. They offer a quality and range of audio-visually illustrated history lessons which individual teachers lacking the resources at the command of these services, cannot compete with save in one important particular. This is the live presence of the teacher in the classroom which makes him more sensitive of the pupils' interests, needs and paces of learning than any sound or television programme can be. Even sound and television broadcasts, excellent though they may be, should be regarded with the pictures, the maps, the film strips and slides, the documents and sound-recordings, as all aids to that central task of the teacher, that of telling the story of history.

The Timetable and the History Room

The amount of time allowed for the study of history and the accommodation available have a considerable effect on the methods employed. Some of the suggestions in this book are only practicable if history has a reasonable allocation of periods in the school while much of the project work and visiting will be easier to undertake if some of the periods can be blocked together. The amount of time permitted for the study of history by school timetables varies greatly from school to school. The liberty which schools enjoy to plan their own allocations of time means that it is impossible to generalize about how much time is available for each age group. Moreover, the presence or absence of a subject in the timetable may not necessarily indicate very clearly the content of the lessons. For instance, a good deal of history may or may not be studied during periods allocated to social studies on the timetable. The only useful figures which are available are those gathered for the Central

Advisory Council for Education when it was preparing its Report on *Half our Future*; these relate to the fourth year in secondary modern schools.

Time given to the study of History and Social Studies

| | Percentage of forms receiving the following number of minutes per week: | | | | | | |
	270–230	225–185	180–140	135–95	90–50	Under 50	Nil
History	—	—	4	23	61	1	11
Social Studies	1	1	4	4	3	4	83

Notes (*a*) In 5 per cent of the forms history is an alternative to some other subject, usually geography.

(*b*) Where social studies occur, it is usually, though not always, as a substitute for history and geography.

The overall impression which these figures convey is that the allocation of time is inadequate in the majority of schools. It is difficult to see how much less than a total of two hours per week can be regarded as sufficient time in which to develop a satisfactory course. The situation is made worse by more recent developments in teaching history for modern methods tend to be more demanding in terms of time. Where it proves to be quite impossible to increase the overall allocation of time for the study of history, some easing of immediate difficulties might be found through a pooling of the history periods with those of another subject similarly situated, often geography. This would yield four or six periods for half of the year first for the one subject, then for the other in place of two or three for each for the whole year, thereby enabling a much more flexible approach to be undertaken to the year's programme in both.

An adequate room in which to teach is just as important as sufficient time. The general-purpose classroom in secondary schools remains well suited to the lecture technique with blackboard illustrations, but it does not offer the facilities which teachers and pupils need if they are to employ the more efficient ways of learning. The equipment needed to teach history to those of modest ability must be permanently housed in the room where history is taught. Sets of books for pupils to consult need to be available during history lessons and so does equipment for model-making, illustrative material such as wall charts and diagrams, projector, tape recorder, gramophone and records. The room itself needs to be rather larger than the average classroom in order to allow plenty of space for the free circulation of pupils when engaged in the more practical activities such as modelling. The facilities offered by a well-equipped history room are essential if teachers and pupils are to give of their best.

7. Examination and Assessment

Examining what a pupil has learned is an essential part of the general educative process. A teacher has first to decide the aim and purpose of his course of lessons and then to devise learning experiences which will enable him to achieve these ends. Some form of examining or assessing follows naturally as a way of enabling both teacher and pupil to test how far the aims have been achieved.

There are special difficulties in carrying out this testing successfully in a number of individual subjects including history. The difficulties here tend to arise from the fact that the overall aim of the history teacher is to achieve certain attitudes of mind in his pupils, to impart certain values or to develop certain qualities through the study of his subject. These attitudes, values or qualities are not readily susceptible to the forms of measurement used in schools; at the same time the amount of factual material remembered is comparatively easily measured. The consequence of this is that in testing history there is a great danger that the testing process will lead to undue emphasis on 'cramming' or the learning of facts simply for the purpose of reproducing them under examination conditions and that this preoccupation will become so overwhelming as to drive out all other aims from the history lesson. In this way much of the value of studying history could be lost.

The extent to which this danger is realized depends largely on the individual teacher. If he has confidence in himself and in the methods which he is using, he is unlikely to fall back on such undesirable practices as the dictation and memorization of notes as a way of preparing his pupils for an examination or test. It is the teacher who is lacking in professional confidence who comes to fear and dread examinations and who falls back on those tricks and devices of the classroom known as 'cramming'. A teacher with this attitude must inevitably infect his pupils with similar fears; very little sound learning is likely to come out of such a classroom situation.

Apart from the ruin that can befall history teaching in a school where the teacher lacks confidence, examining and assessing in history has certain technical difficulties. The nature of the subject has led to the predominance of the essay type of question in examinations. This type of examination presents considerable problems of consistency and reliability. Experience has shown that candidates' papers are valued differently by different examiners or even by the same examiner at different times. The reasons for these variations are numerous, examiners tend to look for different qualities, some may lay great stress on originality, others on knowledge of the subject-matter, or clarity of expression or evidence of interest and wide reading; again there are examiners who are biased in favour of the student who agrees with them while others may mark up the candidate who disagrees.

There is no known way of achieving absolute reliability or consistency in marking essay-type answers. The variations can be greatly reduced if a teacher prepares his marking scheme with considerable care when he sets the question paper and if he will also eliminate from the paper questions which look as though they may present special marking difficulties. The marking scheme should not only indicate how many marks will be allocated to each question but also how many are to be awarded for different parts of each answer. Many teachers find that they are able to establish and maintain a standard more satisfactorily if they mark all the answers to one question before they proceed to another. Marking is above all else a matter of arranging scripts in an order of merit; it therefore helps to read a number of answers first to get a rough idea of the range, then to pick out the best, an average and the poorest answers and mark them accordingly, then rate all the other examples by comparison with these samples.

The actual form in which essay questions are set can help greatly with the marking; moreover, the less able the pupils, the more important it is to phrase the questions in such a way as to provide as much help as possible. Thus rather than asking pupils to 'Write an account of how the barbarian tribes over-ran the Western Roman Empire' it would be much sounder to ask them to 'State which tribes invaded the Western Roman Empire, where did they settle and who were their leaders?'

Another way of modifying the essay type of question so as both to improve the reliability of the marking and to enable pupils of moderate ability to attempt it with a measure of success is to give some of the main points that should be referred to in the answer:

Using the following material, explain what the Poor Law Amendment Act of 1834 did.

The Speenhamland System; the Report of the Poor Law Commission of 1834; ending of outdoor relief for the able bodied; hard conditions in workhouses; grouping of parishes into 'Unions'; unpopularity of the Commissioners; different effects of the Act in agricultural and manufacturing districts.

Another example of the same type of question but this time requiring no more that a paragraph by way of answer might be:

Explain the figures given below:

LONDON TO YORK (by stage-coach)

| 1725 | 36 hours | 1785 | 24 hours |
| 1760 | 32 hours | 1815 | 18 hours |

The difficulty which many children experience when they are expected to write continuous prose in itself limits the value of the essay-type of answer. Consequently many history teachers endeavour to develop types of question which will enable pupils of little literary ability to show their understanding of the history they have been studying:

Write short sentences using correctly SIX of the following:
- (a) Trial by ordeal.
- (b) Pilgrimage.
- (c) Monastic order.
- (d) Court of Pie-powder.
- (e) Oath of fealty.
- (f) Excommunication.
- (g) Villeinage.
- (h) Heresy.

Answer FOUR of the following, explaining in two or three lines what is the link between the events given:
- (a) The Irish Land League's 'Moonlighter' campaign.
  The Coercion Act, 1881.
- (b) The building of the Crystal Palace in Hyde Park.
  The Great Exhibition of 1851.
- (c) Foundation of the Tariff Reform League in 1903.
  The General Election of 1906.

69

(*d*) The outbreak of War in 1914.
The revival of prosperity in English agriculture.
(*e*) Rejection by the House of Lords of the Budget of 1909.
The Parliament Act, 1911.
(*f*) World Economic Crisis, 1931.
MacDonald's National Government, 1931–35.

In devising questions requiring a minimum facility to write continuous prose it is easy to reach the point where recall of fact alone is being tested while understanding is ignored. Such a criticism can be made of the following type of question:

Choose SIX of the following dates and write beside each an important event you associate with it:

1832	1840	1846	1848	1856	1857
1870	1884	1889	1906	1911	1914

The various difficulties presented by questions which require pupils to write their answers has led in some subjects to a movement towards the use of objective tests. Since these tests consist of questions to which there is only one correct answer no subjective element can enter into the marking, absolute consistency can be maintained. The absence of a need for candidates to write continuous prose and consistency in marking can be very important advantages. If sufficient care is taken in preparing the tests, it is usually possible to ensure that they do examine understanding rather than simply powers of recall. On the other hand they cannot test as well as essay questions the ability to argue a case and to present evidence in support of it. Certainly the objective test has not become popular with those who teach and examine history.

Examples of objective-type questions:

1. Which word in each of the following groups is out of place?
(*a*) Kay, Hargreaves, Arkwright, Townshend, Crompton.
(*b*) Telford, Newcomen, Watt, Boulton, Murdock.
(*c*) Ernest Bevin, Neville Chamberlain, Clement Attlee, Stanley Baldwin, Winston Churchill.
(*d*) Perpendicular, Romanesque, Early English, Clerestory, Decorated.
(*e*) Cardinal, Bishop, Abbey, Prior, Deacon.

2. Arrange the following in the order in which they happened:
(*a*) Death of Stalin.
(*b*) Korean War.
(*c*) Versailles Peace Conference.
(*d*) Invasion of Poland by Nazi Germany.
(*e*) Outbreak of the Spanish Civil War.
(*f*) Dropping of the atomic bomb on Hiroshima.
(*g*) War between China and India.

3. Enter FIVE of the following in the correct space on the time-chart:
Discovery of the New World by Columbus; accession of King
Canute; Peasants' Revolt; Coronation of Charlemagne; capture
of Constantinople by the Turks; Magna Carta; landing of St.
Augustine in Kent; Battle of Crecy; the visions of Mohammed;
Simon de Montfort's Parliament.

DATE	EVENTS
500— 599	
600— 699	
700— 799	
800— 899	
900— 999	
1000—1099	
1100—1199	
1200—1299	
1300—1399	
1400—1499	

The difficulties involved in examining history formally have been an
important factor in causing many to favour increasing reliance on the
assessment of course work rather than examination papers in the
Certificate of Secondary Education. Some feel that assessment of
course work can be less 'judicial' or 'impartial' than marking examinations and that the mark or grade given may be dangerously subjective. In practice, the C.S.E. history panels tend to rely upon a
mixture of essay-type questions, objective test questions and course
work assessment and in this way attempt to guard against the weaknesses which might arise from relying on any single form of measuring.

There is, of course, a considerable contrast between this C.S.E. approach and the traditional G.C.E. 'O' level history paper relying on essay-type answers. The new examination has given an opportunity to history teachers to think again about the right way of judging work in their subject for a public award. In thinking about this they have clearly had to bear in mind the notorious difficulties which many boys and girls of no more than average ability have in doing justice to themselves through the medium of the essay. In operating forms of examination and testing for those pupils who are of less than average ability teachers need to have regard to the strengths and weaknesses of the different types of question and to manipulate them in such a way as to encourage learning rather than alarm or depression. For boys and girls who will never seek any form of public academic award, however modest, the only real justification for the test or examination in history must be that it aids or encourages learning and it needs to be adapted accordingly.

PLATE IX

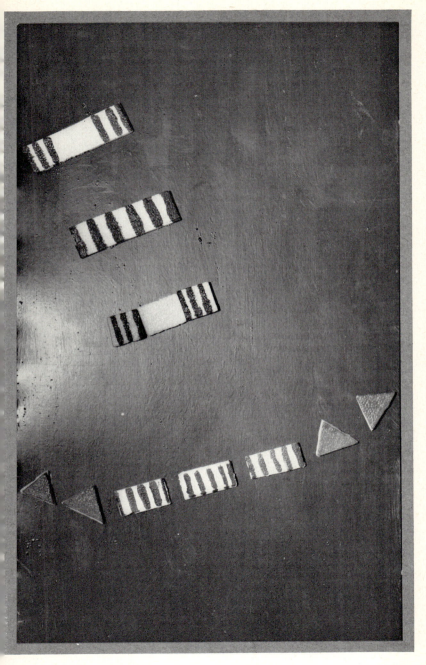

PLATE IX: Magnetic board used here to show movement in the Battle of Agincourt. Above shows alignment of the armies at the start of the battle, French above, English below (*see over page*)

PLATE X: Shows the armies manœuvring at a later stage (*see page* 63)

PLATE X

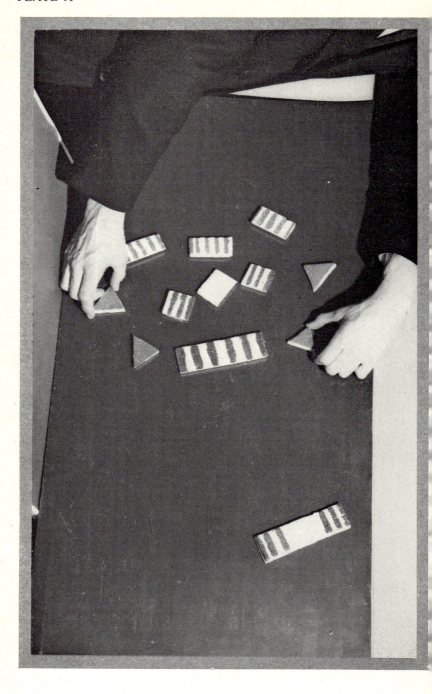

PLATE XI

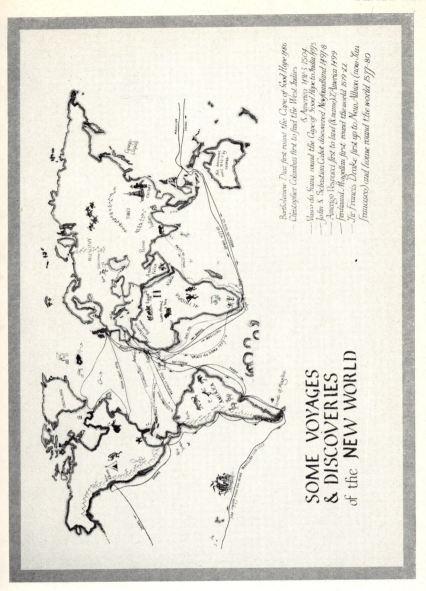

SOME VOYAGES
& DISCOVERIES
of the NEW WORLD

Bartholomew Diaz first round the Cape of Good Hope 1486
Christopher Columbus first to find the West Indies
& America 1492-3 1504
.... Vasco da Gama round the Cape of Good Hope to India 1495
——— John & Sebastian Cabot discovered Newfoundland 1498
——— Amerigo Vespucci first to land (Named) America 1499
——— Ferdinand Magellan first round the world 1519-22
——— Sir Francis Drake first up to New Albion (now San
Francisco) and home round the world 1577-80

PLATE XI and PLATE XII (over page): Examples of work completed by 13 year-old pupils described in Appendix I—'"Patch" on the Elizabethan Age' (*see page* 73)

PLATE XII

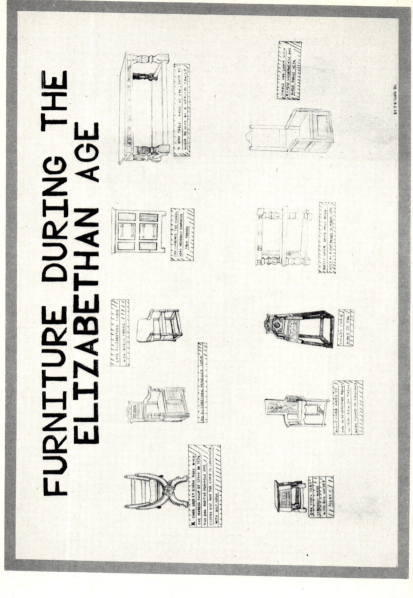

FURNITURE DURING THE ELIZABETHAN AGE

PLATE XIII

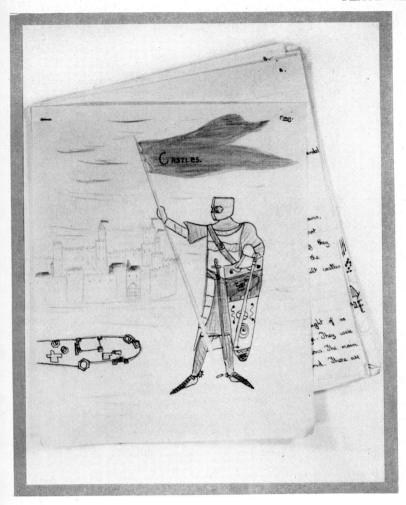

PLATES XIII–XVI: Examples of small books compiled by individual 12 year-old pupils, described in Appendix I—'Individual Work on the Middle Ages' (*see page* 74)

PLATE XIV

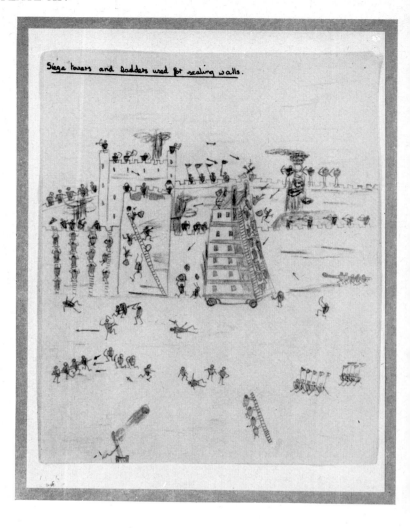

Siege towers and ladders used for scaling walls.

PLATE XV

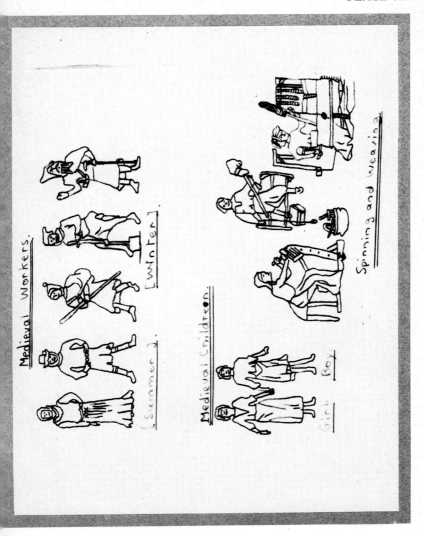

Medieval Workers.

[Summer.] [Winter.]

Medieval Children.

Girl. Boy.

Spinning and weaving.

PLATE XVI

Mediaeval Furniture

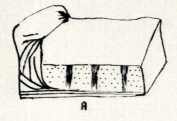

A

B

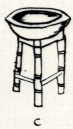

C

A : Couch
B : Bath
C : Bowl & washstand

Appendix I—Children's Work

1. 'Patch' on the Elizabethan Age

This work was undertaken by a class of 13-year-old boys. After the teacher had taken some introductory lessons on the period outlining its main features, the pupils were given the opportunity to find out more about the period for themselves. By a process of pupil choice and teacher guidance each pupil eventually decided upon one of the following subjects as his centre of interest.

Ships and Sailing	Arms and Weapons
Clothes	The Armada
English Explorers	Mary Queen of Scots and the
Spanish Explorers	Catholics
Portuguese Explorers	The Puritans
Games of the sixteenth century	Tortures and Punishments
Plays and Theatres	Wool and Cloth Trade
Schools and Learning	Transport
Trade and Trading Companies	Doctors, Medicine and Diseases
Tudor Money and Prices	Food and Meals ⎫ one pupil
Architecture	Festivals and ⎬ tackled all
Furniture	Holidays ⎭ of these
Drake	Hawkins and the Slave Trade
Raleigh	Town Life

Note. 1. Some of the subjects were very popular, therefore more than one pupil was encouraged to work upon them, either to produce co-operative pieces of work or individual studies.

2. The teacher failed to find anyone in this particular class who would find out about 'Music and Musicians'.

The class were given lesson time and homework time for the next four weeks for this work and they were expected to produce either a booklet or a chart (or both) on their chosen subject.

The teacher's role in this work was one of guidance. Before the work began he gave the class a good deal of help on where they could find out about their topics. A lesson was held in the History Room and the pupils were re-introduced to the History Library housed there. It was not a large library but the following books were pointed out as 'some useful ones to start with . . . now look for others'.

History of Everyday Things, Vol. 2, Quennell (Batsford)
Picture Source Book of the 16th Century, Harrison (Allen & Unwin)
Spacious Days of Queen Elizabeth (Rockliffe Project Series)
Life in Shakespeare's England, Dover Wilson (Pelican)
English Seamen, Sellman (Methuen)
They Saw it Happen, Vol. 2 (Blackwell)

The pupils were then encouraged to search the School Library and the local Public Libraries. In the course of the next four weeks the teacher was bombarded with questions about selection and presentation of the material that many of the pupils (though not all!) had eagerly found. Finally, the teacher tried to integrate all this work by arranging a classroom exhibition of all the visual material, by encouraging the circulation around the class of all the various booklets which were produced and allowing time for them to be read, by letting some of the pupils give five-minute lecturettes on their subjects, and by organizing a Brains Trust in which the class found out from each other about various aspects of the period.

Some of the charts produced for this 'patch' are shown on Plates XI and XII.

2. Individual Work on the Middle Ages

This work was undertaken by a class of 12-year-olds. The period from 1066 to 1485 had been studied for the previous two terms in a variety of ways, now the pupils had the opportunity to take some topic which particularly interested them, find out about it in more detail, and then produce their own book on the subject.

Small books, from which there are illustrations on Plates XIII–XVI were produced on the following topics:

Town Life through the Ages, first century B.C. to sixteenth century A.D.
Chivalry 1154–1485.
Architecture.
The Medieval Tournament.

Great Names of Norman England.
Early Writers.
Ships, Seamen and Exploration.
The Early History of the Church in England.
Early Musical Instruments.
Castles and Fortresses.
Medieval English Warfare.
The Crusades.
Cathedrals.
Heraldry.
Magna Carta (not a success!).
The Black Death.
The Medieval Monastery.
The Battle of Hastings.

3. A 'Domesday Inquiry'

The following extracts are the work of 7–8 year-olds, but the exercise set and the results are not without interest for the secondary school teacher, particularly in this period of reorganization when 'middle-schools' are beginning to emerge.

In an attempt to get the children to imagine what the Domesday Inquiry of 1086 really entailed, as part of their work on this subject they were set the following exercise:

'Imagine the Queen and the Prime Minister have asked you to write down what your household consists of today in 1966.'

Below are some of the results.

1. I live at 1 Lyndon Grove. I have a brother named Graham, he is 13 years old. Our gran lives with us. In our garden we have a swing, shed, garage and two lawns. We also grow flowers and vegetables in our garden. Inside the house there is a kitchen and a living-room. Upstairs there are three bedrooms and a bathroom.
2. I live in a house.
   I have a brother and sister.
   I have no pets.
   I have a mommy and daddy.
   My garden is concrete.
   My daddy as got a van.

F*

3. I have five brothers and one sister.
   My sister has a poodle and my brother has a cat.
   We have potatos in our garden.
   We will soon have letace and peas in our garden soon.
   My brothers' names are Nigel, Adrian, Jan and of course myself
   and my sisters name is Denise.
4. In the house and in the garden

Mother	daffodils
father	tulips
sister	dog
garden	mouse
shed	fish
roses	chairs
primroses	tables
	carpets.

Some examples of work with documentary material discussed in Chapter 4

DOMESDAY BOOK

I. *The Anglo-Saxon Chronicle tells us about the Survey*

1085 Then at Christmas, the King was at Gloucester with his council
... and the King had much thought with his council about this
country—how it was occupied or with what sort of people. Then
he sent his men over all England into every shire and had them
find out what land the King held and what taxes he ought to
have every year from the shire ... how much everybody had
who was occupying land in England, in land or cattle and how
much money it was worth.... The investigation was so
thorough that there was not a yard of land nor one ox nor one
cow nor one pig left out of the record. Then all the records
were brought to him.

1. Why do you think King William wanted the survey?
   Can you suggest three different reasons why he wanted it?
2. Do you think the Anglo-Saxon monk who wrote the Chronicle
   would be in favour of the survey?
   Imagine you are such a monk and write a letter to a friend
   expressing your views about it.

II. *The first part of the record of the Ely Enquiry tells us:*

(*a*)   *How the Enquiry was made*
'Here is written down . . . the way in which the King's barons made their enquiries, namely by oath of the sherriff of the shire and of all the barons and of their French tenants, of the priest, the reeve and six villagers of each village.'

(*b*)   *What questions were asked*
'They asked the name of the manor, who held it in the time of King Edward, who holds it now, the number of hides (areas) of land, the number of ploughs, the number of villagers, the amount of forest, the amount of meadow, the number of milk cows, the number of fish ponds . . . how much it was worth in the time of King Edward, at the time when King William gave it, and how much it is worth now, and if more can be got out of it than is done so already.'

1.   Write down a list of questions you think a modern Domesday investigator might ask if he visited a farm today.

2.   Write, act and arrange an Enquiry as described in (*a*) above.

III. *The entry in Domesday Book for Leeds*

In Leeds 10 carucates of land (that is, land for 10 ploughs) and 6 oxgangs to be taxed. Land to 6 ploughs. 7 Thanes held in the time of King Edward for 7 manors.
27 villeins and 4 sokemen and 4 borders have now there 14 ploughs.
There is a priest and a church and a mill of 4 shillings and 10 acres of meadows.
It has been valued at 6 pounds, now 7 pounds.

1.   Work out the population figures for Leeds from this record in
(*a*) number of households (each number represents the number of households, e.g. there were 4 sokemen's households)
(*b*) number of people (for this multiply the number of households by 5)

2.   Draw a map of Leeds as it might have been in 1086 from the information given, plot the mill, the church, the meadow land (near the river) and the 'various' houses.

IV. *The entry in Domesday Book for Bradford*

In Bradford Gamel had 15 hides where 8 ploughs can be.
Ilbert has it, and it is waste.

In the time of King Edward it was worth £4.

1. The Bradford entry tells us in two ways that once it had been a prosperous area but later in 1086 it was a poor area. Can you find these two clues?

2. Can you find out why Bradford was not so prosperous in 1086 as it had been in 1066? What had William done to much of the North in between these dates?

N.B. In the Victoria County History for each county, there is a translation of the relevant portion of Domesday Book. Entries are listed under landowners starting with the King and ending with the smallest tenant-in-chief. It can be used to plot the manors which any one tenant held in the county, e.g. in group work, one group could plot the King's manors, another group a bishop's manors, etc.

Appendix II—Source Material and Bibliography

A few books about different approaches to History Teaching

Bell, J. J., *History in Schools* (Wheaton, 1964).

Burston, W. H. and Green, C. W., *A Handbook for History Teachers* (Methuen, 1962).

Burston, W. H. and Thompson, D., *Studies in the Nature and Teaching of History* (Routledge & Kegan Paul, 1967).

Carpenter, P., *The Era Approach* (Cambridge University Press, 1965).

Fairley, J. A., *Activity Methods in History* (Nelson, 1967).

Happold, F. C., *The Approach to History* (Christophers, 1950).

Hemming, J., *The Teaching of Social Studies in Secondary Schools* (Longmans, 1951).

I.A.A.M., *The Teaching of History* (Cambridge University Press, 3rd ed., 1965).

Jeffreys, M. V. C., *History in Schools: the Study of Development* (Pitman, 1939).

Lewis E. M., *Teaching History in Secondary Schools* (Evans 1965).

Ministry of Education, Department of Education and Science.
Pamphlet No. 23: *The Teaching of History* (H.M.S.O. 1952).
Pamphlet No. 52: *Towards World History* (H.M.S.O. 1967).

The Historical Association (59a Kennington Park Road, London, S.E.11)

This is the only national association concerned with history teaching. It has local branches in most of the larger towns and cities which consist largely of teachers who concern themselves both with the further study of history and with the problems involved in teaching in schools. Until the Second World War the teaching interest was directed almost exclusively towards grammar schools, but since then the Association has widened its interests and has published pamphlets on various aspects of history teaching in all types of secondary schools. Full details of the publications currently available may be obtained from the Honorary Secretary to the Association at the above address, but a few are listed below to give some idea of the scope of those available.

79

Teaching of History Committee Pamphlets:

No. 4, *Russia—Notes on a Course for Secondary Schools* by P. D. Whitting, revised 1966.

No. 5, *The U.S.A.—Notes on a Course for Secondary Schools* by C. P. Hill and P. J. Harris, revised 1967.

No. 6, *The Museum and the School,* by M. E. Bryant, revised edition.

No. 8, *The History of London; Notes on a Course for Secondary Modern Schools,* by M. Honeybourne.

No. 18, *Recent Historical Fiction for Secondary School Children (11–15 years),* by Kenneth Charlton.

No. 21, *The Teaching of History in Secondary Schools,* by F. J. Dwyer.

No. 22, *Coins in the Classroom, An Introduction to Numismatics for Teachers,* by P. D. Whitting.

Some helpful books for use in teaching Local History

Kullicke, F. W. and Emmison, F. G., *English Local History Handlist* (Historical Association, 1965).
Valuable bibliography and list of sources.

Douch, R., *Local History and the Teacher* (Routledge & Kegan Paul, 1967).

Douch, R. and Steer, F. W., *Local History Essays: Some Notes for Students* (University of Southampton Institute of Education).

Emmison, F. G., *Archives and Local History* (Methuen, 1966).

Emmison, F. G. and Gray, I., *County Records* (Historical Association, 1961).

Hoskins, W. G., *Local History in England* (Longmans, 1959).

West, J., *Village Records* (Macmillan, 1966).
The Historian's Guide to Ordnance Survey Maps (National Council of Social Service, 1964).

Short Guides to Records

A series of leaflets obtainable from the Historical Association, single copies 6d. each plus postage, 25 for 8s. 6d., 100 for 30s. There are available short guides to the use of: Rate Books, Poll Books, Probate Inventories, Estate Maps and Surveys, Guardians' Minute Books, Chantry Certificates, Hearth Tax Returns, Episcopal Visitation Books, Estate Acts of Parliament, Wills, Recusant Rolls, Deeds of Title, Glebe Terriers, Enclosure Awards and Acts, Records of Commissions of Sewers, Land Tax Assessment, Parliamentary Surveys, Turnpike Records.

Copies of Domesday Book entries may be obtained from the Public Record Office; write to the Secretary, Public Record Office, Chancery Lane, London, W.C.2, for an order form.

Air photographs of selected localities may be obtained from the Air Photography Officer, Room 11/4, Ministry of Housing and Local Government, Whitehall, London, S.W.1., sending grid references and a note of the purpose for which required.

Reference Books mainly for use by Pupils in the 'Patch' (or 'Era') and project approaches to history

The list below is of reference for information books which are often suitable for children who are finding out for themselves historical information. Catalogues from the publishers should be consulted to find out the extent of the series of books listed. The list is in alphabetical order of publishers.

A.D. Historical News Sheets.
    Allen & Unwin, 40 Museum Street, London, W.C.1.
Picture Source Books for Social History.
    Allen & Unwin.
Understanding the Modern World.
    Allen & Unwin.
The St. George's Library (e.g. Rome, Ancient Greece, Medicine).
    Edward Arnold Ltd., 41 Maddox Street, London, W.1.
The Rockliff New Project Histories (background booklets, practical books).
    Barrie & Rockliff, 2 Clement's Inn, Strand, London, W.C.2.
Junior Heritage Books.
    B. T. Batsford Ltd., 4 Fitzhardinge Street, London, W.1.
A History of Everyday Things in England (4 vols.) M. and C. H. B. Quennell.
    B. T. Batsford Ltd.
Everyday Life and Everyday Things (e.g. Prehistoric Times, Roman and Saxon Times, New Testament Times, Ancient Greece).
    B. T. Batsford Ltd.
English Life Series, ed. P. Quennell.
    B. T. Batsford Ltd.
Past into Present Series (e.g. Transport, Law and Order).
    B. T. Batsford Ltd.
Black's Junior Reference Books, ed. R. J. Unstead.
    A. & C. Black, 4–6 Soho Square, London, W.1.

Looking at History Series, ed. R. J. Unstead.
  A. & C. Black.
Social Life in England, John Finnemore.
  A. & C. Black.
They Saw it Happen (4 vols), 55 B.C.–1945. A very valuable series of extracts.
  Blackwell & Mott Ltd., 49 Broad Street, Oxford.
How They Lived.
  Basil Blackwell.
Blackwell's Pocket Histories.
  Basil Blackwell.
The Study Books, ed. Ray Mitchell.
  The Bodley Head Ltd., 10 Earlham Street, London, W.C.2.
World Culture Series.
  Brockhampton Press Ltd., Market Place, Leicester.
Journeys through Our Early History, ed. Colin Clair.
  Bruce & Gawthorn Ltd., 21–23 Market Street, Watford, Herts.
What was Their Life?, ed. Raymond Fawcett.
  Bruce & Gawthorn.
Man and his Conquests.
  Burke Publishing Co. Ltd., 14 John Street, London, W.C.1.
Jackdaws, ed. John Langdon Davies.
  Jonathan Cape Ltd., 30 Bedford Square, London, W.C.1.
Cassell Caravel Books.
  Cassell & Co. Ltd., 35 Red Lion Square, London, W.C.1.
Dawn of History, Richard Carrington.
  Chatto & Windus Ltd., 40–42 William IV St., London, W.C.2.
Studies in English History, G. R. Kesteven.
  Chatto & Windus.
The Bayeux Tapestry, N. Denny and Filmer Sankey.
  Collins, 14 St James's London S.W.1.
How Things Developed Books.
  Educational Supply Association, 233 Shaftesbury Avenue, London, W.C.2.
The Story of . . . , Agnes Allen.
  Faber & Faber, Ltd., 24 Russell Square, London, W.C.1.
History Bookshelves and *Museum Bookshelves* (sets of 6 booklets), ed. Catherine B. Firth.
  Ginn & Co. Ltd., 18 Bedford Row, London, W.C.1.

Look Books.
Hamish Hamilton, 90 Great Russell Street, London, W.C.1.
This Wonderful World.
George G. Harrap & Co. Ltd., 182 High Holborn, London, W.C.1.
Meals Through the Ages, Sports and Pastimes Through the Ages, Our Own Homes Through the Ages, Peter Moss.
Harrap.
Great Civilizations, C. A. Burland.
Hulton Educational Publications Ltd., 55–59 Saffron Hill, London, E.C.1.
Children in History (5 books), Molly Harrison.
Hulton.
Portraits and Documents, ed. J. S. Millward.
Hutchinson Educational Ltd., 178–202 Great Portland Street, London, W.1.
The New Illustrated History of Science and Inventions (vols. on Medicine, Ships, Flights, Weapons, etc.).
Leisure Arts, Ltd., London.
Then and There, ed. M. Reeves.
Longmans Green & Co. Ltd., 48 Grosvenor Street, London, W.1.
Man's Heritage, ed. E. H. Dance.
Longmans.
Evidence in Pictures, Islay Doncaster.
Longmans.
Story of Britain in Pictures (6 books).
Thomas Hope & Sankey Hudson Ltd., Manchester (or Woolworths).
The Wonderful World (Rathbone Books).
Macdonald & Co. Ltd., 2 Portman Street, London W.1.
History Picture Books, ed. E. J. S. Lay.
Macmillan & Co. Ltd., St. Martin's Street, London, W.C.2.
Methuen's Outlines, ed. Patrick Thornhill.
Methuen & Co. Ltd., 11 New Fetter Lane, London, E.C.4.
Exploring the Past, ed. E. Royston Pike.
Frederick Muller Ltd., 110 Fleet Street, London, E.C.4.
True Books, ed. Vernon Knowles (Castles, Ships, Costumes).
Muller.
The Changing Shape of Things (e.g. Transport by Land, Sea, Air; Dress; Food.
John Murray, 50 Albemarle Street, London, W.1.

Longacre Book of Ships, etc.
   Odhams Press, 40 Long Acre, London, W.C.2.
Quest Library.
   Oliver & Boyd Ltd., Tweeddale Court, Edinburgh 1.
The Signpost Library.
   Oliver & Boyd.
How They were Built, J. Stewart Murphy.
   Oxford University Press, Amen House, Warwick Square, London, E.C.4.
Oxford Junior Encyclopaedia.
   Oxford University Press.
People of the Past, ed. Philippa Pearce.
   Oxford University Press.
A New Look at World History, M. Neurath and J. A. Lauwerys.
   Max Parrish & Co. Ltd., 55 Queen Anne Street, London, W.1.
Penguin Books, various, as Puffins, King Penguins, Pelicans.
English History in Pictures, The Historical Association.
   George Philip & Son Ltd., Victoria Road, London, N.W.10.
How Series, ed. Phoebe Snow.
   Routledge & Kegan Paul Ltd., Broadway House, 68–74 Carter Lane, London, E.C.4.
Visual History of Modern Britain, ed. Jack Simmons.
   Studio Vista Ltd., Blue Star House, Highgate Hill, London, N.19.
The Discovery Reference Books, ed. Alys L. Gregory.
   University of London Press Ltd., Little Paul's House, Warwick Square, London, E.C.4.
First Books.
   Edmund Ward, 194–200 Bishopsgate, London, E.C.2.
How to Explore (Information Books).
   Ward Lock Educational Co. Ltd., 116 Baker St., London, W.1.
How Things Developed (Information Books).
   Ward Lock.
The Young Historian, ed. Patrick Moore.
   Weidenfeld & Nicolson (Educational) Ltd., 20 New Bond Street, London, W.1.
The Wheaton Junior Reference Books.
   A. Wheaton & Co. Ltd., Fore Street, Exeter.

Some Gramophone Records of use in the teaching of history

TITLE	COMPANY	NUMBER
King John and Magna Carta	Columbia	335X.1718 Mono.

TITLE	COMPANY	NUMBER
Oliver Cromwell	H.M.V.	XLP 40003
Elizabeth the Great	H.M.V.	XLP 40005
Abraham Lincoln	H.M.V.	XLP 40004
Churchill—Wartime Speeches	{ H.M.V.	ALP 1435–6
	{ H.M.V.	ALP 1556–63
B.B.C. Scrapbook Programmes		
1914		493 015 FDL
1940		493 014 FDL
1945		493 016 FDL
Easter Week and After The nationalist movement in Ireland, 1916 partition, the I.R.A. etc.	Topic	12T 44
Jacobite Rebellions Fairly full historical note included.	Topic	12T 79
Steam Whistle Ballads English and Scottish social and industrial history.	Topic	12T 104
Ireland Her Own Irish nationalism.	Topic	12T 153
Frost and Fire English social history and folklore, pagan survivals.	Topic	12T 136
The Iron Muse Much as 12T 104 but better programmed and the different singers used make the record more attractive for children.	Topic	12T 86
Farewell Nancy Sea Shanties	Topic	12T 110
Blow the Man Down Sea Shanties	Topic	TOP 98
A Hundred Years Ago Sea Shanties	Topic	TOP 99
The Coast of Peru Sea Shanties	Topic	TOP 100
Tommy Armstrong of Tyneside Social life of Tyneside and environs, could lead into	Topic	12T 122

TITLE	COMPANY	NUMBER
examination of impact of Industrial Revolution on an area with its own traditions.		
The Collier's Rant	Topic	TOP 74
Mining songs of the Northumberland and Durham coalfields.		
Modern Times—a Series of Books and Records.	Longmans	
Titles include World War I, Franco and the Spanish Civil War, Hitler and Germany, Mussolini and Italy, Roosevelt and the United States.		

Some addresses for useful Teaching Aids.

British Insurance Association, Aldermary House, Queen Street, London, E.C.4.
Films on free loan. Free booklet 'The Story of British Insurance'. Wall charts and film strip free.

British Steel Corporation, Steel House, Tothill Street, London, S.W.1.
Films on free loan. Slides for loan or for sale. Booklets, individual copies free.

British Sugar Bureau, 140 Park Lane, London W.1.
Requests for material should be addressed to Educational Productions Ltd., East Ardsley, Wakefield, Yorkshire.

British Wool Marketing Board, Education Department, Oak Mills, Clayton, Bradford, Yorkshire.
Booklets for sale, e.g.: 'Wool in History', 'Wool through the Ages'. Also wall sheets.

Brooke Bond Education Service, Heathrow House, Bath Road, Cranford, Hounslow, Middx.
Booklets for sale: 'Story of Tea', 'Story of Coffee'. Also film strips, picture cards and booklets such as 'The History of British Costume', and wall charts for sale and films on free loan.

Cadbury Brothers Limited, Schools Department, Bournville, Birmingham.

Booklets, project notes, friezes, wall charts for sale. Film strips on free loan.

Ceylon Tea Centre, 22 Regent Street, London, S.W.1.

Various booklets, posters, maps and project material for sale. Films on free loan.

Dunlop Company Limited, The Education Section, 10–12 King Street, London, S.W.1.

Free booklets up to 20 copies of each booklet: 'This is where Rubber Begins', 'Treasure in the House' (Story of English Furniture), 'Story of the Wheel', 'Story of the Ship', 'The Story of Flight', 'The Quickest Way' (Story of Transport). Also films on free loan from Dunlop Film Library, Wilton Crescent, Merton Park, London, S.W.19, and film strips and wall charts for sale.

Hudson's Bay Company, Beaver House, Great Trinity Lane, London, E.C.4.

Free booklet, 'A Brief History of the Hudson's Bay Company'. Film strip on the history of the Company on free loan or purchase from Unicorn Head Production Limited, 42 Westminster Palace Gardens, Artillery Row, London, S.W.1.

National Coal Board Publications, Hobart House, Grosvenor Place, London, S.W.1.

Various booklets and leaflets.

National Dairy Council, National Dairy Centre, 145 Charing Cross Road, London, W.C.2.

Booklets and charts for sale, e.g. 'History of Milk', 'Churns and Cheeses'—a short History of Milk and Cheese.

Petroleum Information Bureau, 4 Brook Street, London, W.1.

Various booklets, one copy of each free.

Guide to Illustrative Material for use in Teaching History.

Published by the Historical Association in 1962 contains much information on other possible teaching materials.

Index